THE BABYLONIAN TALMUD

THE BABYLONIAN
TALMUD
IN SELECTION

Edited and translated from the original
Hebrew and Aramaic by
LEO AUERBACH

PHILOSOPHICAL LIBRARY
NEW YORK

ISBN 978-0-8022-0045-7

Printed in the U. S. A.

CONTENTS

THE STORY OF THE TALMUD

INTRODUCTION

THE word Talmud means study. The *Talmud* is a record of about a thousand years of accumulated Jewish learning and wisdom in all fields of endeavor: Law, religion, ethics, history, science and folklore.

This lore is called Oral Law, in contra-distinction to the *Bible,* which is the Written Law. Tradition has it that this Oral Law was indicated to Moses and handed down by him to future generations; in each generation the great teachers of the period in turn handed it down, amplified but still in oral form, to the next generation.

Early in the history of the Jewish people it was found necessary to expound and interpret the laws as given by Moses; this law-giver himself appointed judges throughout Israel for this very purpose. Particularly true was this after the return of the Jews from Babylonian captivity, when, through the effort of Ezra, the *Torah* became the law and the guiding spirit of all the people. Its reading in public three times a week, with explanations and translations into Aramaic (the vernacular of the people), was at this time made mandatory.

The transgression of the laws was severely punished by the court or by "death at the hands of the Lord". However, life in this new Jewish society was more complex than in the olden days. Some of the laws became obsolete, while others had to be reinterpreted to conform to new conditions.

The *Torah,* however, was the Law, which could not be altered. Therefore the scribes and the members of the Great Assembly busied themselves in probing and searching every sentence and every word of the Scriptures, to find solutions to the vexing problems by interpretations of each law. This method of analysis and exposition was called from the Hebrew word *darash,* to search, to probe, *Midrash.*

The *Midrashim* are of two kinds. Some are concerned with the strict and terse interpretation of the laws and statutes as found in the Scriptures, mainly in *Exodus, Leviticus,* and *Deuteronomy.* These are called *Halachoth.* The others, called *Haggadoth,* are homiletic in style; they took as their topic the narrative parts of the Bible and used them as vehicles for the expounding of ethical precepts, proverbs, parables, and history.

It was the custom to recite a passage of the Scriptures, which served as a thread upon which the expounder could string all sorts of interpretations, and by skillful and often dialectic argumentation, make the law serve new essential purposes. Thus the Law was kept effective in the life of the community, its scope widened as society grew complex.

Particularly popular with the people were the *Haggadic Midrashim.* These were especially adaptable to preaching in the Synagogues or the great open-air gatherings. On several occasions, however, the sages voiced opposition to the *Haggadah,* particularly to those parts that are given to exaggeration and triviality; nonetheless, they also recognized its charm for the masses and its great moral force, and accorded it to the same importance as the *Halachah.*

The great teachers of antiquity among the Hebrews were the scribes, to whom many of the earlier *Midrashic* interpretations could probably be traced. They flourished for some two centuries after 500 B.C. and were followed by the Pharisees who headed the Sanhedrin. The Pharisees were more lenient and liberal in their interpretations of the laws than the Saducees, the aristocrats who adhered to a more literal and strict interpretation of the Scriptures, and therefore the Pharisees were more popular with the people and exerted a greater influence as the dominating force in the life of Jewry. Their influence became even greater as the government and the degenerating aristrocracy became corrupt and oppressed the people.

The first chapter of the tractate *Aboth,* Fathers of the Mishnah, traces the chronological order of these great teachers. The most prominent of them was Hillel, the Prince. He headed the contingent of the Sages who were known as the House of Hillel. These were opposed by Shamai and his colleagues. Their strife evoked a great interest in the contemporary Jewish world, but, as the rivalry was purely intellectual, it spurred them on to greater activity, and fostered learning.

Hillel, who advocated a wider and more liberal application of laws, was invariably successful in having his laws adopted. He was the author of the law known as

Prosbul (before the court). According to the "Law of the Seventh year" *Deuteronomy* XV, all indebtedness became automatically cancelled in the sabbatical year. Because of this law, the rich refused to lend money to the traders and that brought stagnation to business. By a very ingenious interpretation of the passages in the Scriptures referring to this law, Hillel was able to devise the enactment of the *Prosbul,* by which a document was executed transferring the debt to the court, thus making the law of the seventh year not applicable to the specified loan. In a similar manner he enacted a law by which a man who sold his house in a walled city could redeem it from the buyer before one year was over, by depositing its value with the court.

Hillel also inaugurated the seven standard methods of scriptural analysis, which were later, by Rabbi Ishmael, increased to thirteen. These methods served as a scientific basis for the study and analysis of the *Torah.* Hillel is also credited with being the first one to make an attempt to collect and arrange the laws in a systematic order.

With the domination of foreign powers and the consequent decline of the government, the Jews rallied more and more around the Sages and their academies. It was with Hillel that the presidency of the Sanhendrin was made hereditary.

Toward the end of the 1st Century B.C. the country was in a deplorable condition, under a weak and decadent government. The puppet kings were tools of the Roman leaders, who through them manipulated the election and controlled the office of the high priests.

The population was torn by the strife of many warring parties within and an enemy from without. The Jews fought bravely, many of their illustrious Sages and the flower of their youth fell on the fields of battle, but they were no match for the powerful and well organized Roman armies. The great Master of this period was Rabbi Yohanan ben Zakai. Foreseeing the tragic end of the struggle against the Romans, he counselled submission, but his advice was unheeded.

One night, smuggled out of the city by his disciples, he presented himself before the Roman commander to ask for permission to establish his academy in Yabneh, and to plead for the safety of its disciples. Upon the fall of Jerusalem, Rabbi Yohanan re-established the Sanhedrin in Yabneh, to which city and its academy the center of Jewish law and thought was transferred.

The Sages realized that with the Temple gone and the Hebrews leaving the world stage as a politically independent nation, it was encumbent upon them to find some standard around which to rally and bind the People of Israel. There were the Scriptures, which long ago Ezra and the scribes had made popular among the people, and the study and worship of which the Pharisees had endeared. Rabbi Yohanan ben Zakai and his followers made it their concern to emphasize the paramount importance of the Bible and its study in the life of the Jews. Rabban Gamaliel II, the legitimate heir to the presidency of the *Sanhedrin,* succeeded Rabbi Yohanan ben Zakai. With his accession, its authority was soon recognized by the Romans and accepted by Jewry within Palestine and without. Rabban Gamaliel II is remembered also for discarding the custom of lavish and excessively ceremonious and costly funerals; he inaugurated the use of the simple pine coffin and plain shroud that still predominate today.

Turbulent conditions forced the seat of the *Sanhedrin* to move from place to place many times, but it survived as an institution until 425 A.D.

This was the most fruitful and far-reaching period in the post-Biblical history of the Jews. The Rabbis succeeded in moulding a unified and homogeneous people out of the remnants of scattered Jewry. They enacted laws, and fostered ideas and ideals. They compiled, arranged, and systematized their many laws, and bequeathed them to future generations in such a manner that most of them have survived and are valid to this day among the Jews throughout the world. Through the Romans and the early Christians these ideas, laws and customs likewise penetrated other cultures. Many of the laws inaugurated in those days form the basis of the laws by which we are guided today.

TALMUDIC LITERATURE

All the interpretations and commentaries on the Law were retained in oral form. Many of the scholars, however, in order to refresh their memories, privately made notes and jotted down some of these laws. There are many collections of the *midrashim*, attributed to different scholars whose names appear in the Talmud. The most important of these collections are:

1. The *Mekilta*, a commentary on the book of *Exodus*, beginning with chapter 12 and ending with the Sabbatical laws in Chapter 35. This is attributed to Rabbi Ishmael, who lived during the first century A.D. There is also a *Mekilta* attributed to Rabbi Yohai.

2. *Sifra,* a *midrashic* interpretation of *Leviticus.* This was probably compiled in the school of Rabbi Akiba, the great sage who was born about 50 A.D. and died as a martyr in 136, during the rebellion of Bar Kochba.

3. *Sifreh*: Two commentaries, one on *Numbers* and one on *Deuteronomy.* These two books were not composed in the same school, but are found linked together from the earliest days. The commentary on *Numbers* is composed almost exclusively of *Halachic Midrashim,* and betrays the method and style of Rabbi Ishmael, while that on *Deuteronomy* is full of *Haggadic Midrashim* and is probably the product of the school of Rabbi Akiba.

As these commentaries grew and multiplied, attempts were made to collect, then to arrange them systematically so that they could be retained in the memory. The pioneer in this work was Rabbi Akiba, who divided the *Halachoth* according to subject: laws dealing with women; civil laws; etc. He also classified them into categories, such as the four primary causes of damage.

Many of the followers and disciples of Rabbi Akiba and Rabbi Ishmael made compilations of their own, the circulation of which brought on confusion.

The great work of compiling and arranging the laws was finally undertaken and accomplished by Rabbi Yehuda, the Prince, often referred to simply as Rabbi. Through his authority as the President of the *Sanhedrin,* he reduced them to writing, codified them and made them valid as the *Mishna,* which means "the repetition of the law." He visited many of the academies and gathered the collections and private notes that were circulated among the teachers of his day, and with the aid of a committee of his academy, established a definitive text.

The *Mishna* was divided into six orders:
1. *ZERAIM,* dealing with agriculture.
2. *MOED,* dealing with festivals.
3. *NASHIM,* pertaining to women.
4. *NEZIKIN,* dealing with civil and criminal law.
5. *KODASHIM,* dealing with sacrifices.
6. *TOHAROTH,* dealing with cleanliness and purifications.

The orders were divided into tractates, sixty-three in all.

The codification of the *Mishna* did not preclude the further study of the Law. There were the *Halachoth* compiled by other Rabbis, which were not included in the *Mishna.* Many of these are cited in the *Talmud,* however, as *Baraithoth* "external."

Many of the disciples of Rabbi, some with his approbation, emulated him in compiling *Mishnas* of their own. One such compilation, ascribed to various of his followers, is the *Thosafta,* which means addenda, but is really an independent work arranged in six orders in the manner of the *Mishna,* containing new and different material.

The Babylonian Talmud

Ever since the destruction of the First Temple and, even for some time preceding it, there was a large Jewish population in Babylonia (modern Iraq). It was concentrated in a few large cities, where they continued to live and prosper as a homogeneous community. Here developed some of the greatest lights of ancient Israel. The prophet Ezekiel lived in Babylonia; Ezra, Nehemiah, and the early scribes all came up from there to rebuild their country and the House of God. Hillel the Prince, together with some of the Sages, was also a Babylonian.

With the Roman conquest in 70 A.D., and later with the suppression of the rebellion of 135 A.D., many scholars were among those who fled thither from Palestine and the sword of the Romans.

Babylon was not despoiled by the Roman warriors. Remote from the war, the Jews remained there in comparative security as a recognized minority headed by the Exiliarch, a descendant of the house of David, empowered by the Babylonian government to decree laws and appoint judges.

The prosperity and liberty enjoyed by the Jews in Babylonia was conducive to intellectual growth; thus the academies established in Babylonia were renowned for their scholarship, and their learning was held in a higher esteem in the fourth and fifth centuries than that of the Palestinian Rabbis.

The most prominent of the Babylonian scholars was Abba Areka, commonly referred to as Rab. He studied under Rabbi Yehuda in Palestine for many years. Upon his return to Babylonia he founded the academy at Sura. Rab and his contemporary Mar Samuel, the head of the academy at Nehadrea, raised the scholarship and reputation of the Babylonian academies to the highest level. Though the supreme authority was vested in the *Sanhedrin* in Palestine, the Babylonian rulings and decisions were invariably accepted and followed. For the sake of national unity, however, the Jews of Babylonia elected to submit to the authority of the Prince and the rulings of the Palestinian *Sanhedrin*.

With the abolition of the Office of the Prince, the dissolution of the *Sanhedrin,* and the disintegration of the Jewish community in Palestine in the 5th century, leadership and authority passed into the hands of the Babylonian Sages.

Towards the end of the fourth century Rab Ashi, the head of the academy in Sura, proceeded to collect the accumulated literature and learning of the post-Mishnaic period. Seminaries called *Kalla* were held at the academy twice a year; a tractate was selected and announced in advance for each *Kalla.* When the scholars and their disciples gathered at the academy, a passage from the *Mishna* tractate was read and discussed. These discussions, recorded, constitute the *Gemara.*

Rab Ashi began the *Gemara* as a literary undertaking for its own sake. Soon, however, Jews in Babylonia were subjected to religious persecution by the Sassanian Kings, who wished to introduce the teachings of Zoroaster. Rabina, the successor of Rab Ashi, concerned over the possible disappearance of the great rabbinic literature, hurriedly edited and codified the *Gemara,* giving it the form it has retained to this day.

In its narrower sense of the term, the word *Talmud* is applied to the *Mishna* and the *Gemara.* In its wider connotation it includes also the *Midrashim,* the *Mekilta,* the *Sifra,* the *Sifreh,* the *Tosefta* and several less important works, already referred to.

The *Babylonian Talmud,* as it has come down to us, is usually printed in its original languages, in Hebrew script, in 22 folio volumes.

The *Palestinian,* or Jerusalem *Talmud,* as it is often

called, is printed in the same manner in from four to eight volumes.

There were very cordial relations and frequent interchange of teachers between the Palestinian and Babylonian academies, so that the names of the same teachers appear in both *Talmuds*. The *Palestinian Talmud*, however, smaller in scope, has exerted little influence on Jewish life as a whole. The *Babylonian Talmud*, on the other hand, has been a constant and basic force in world Jewry, down to this very day. So potent has its influence been, that Jewry has had to guard against a tendency to accept all its statements as law. As the noted Christian Talmudic scholar, Herman L. Strack points out:* "The Talmud is not a law book, not a code, in which every sentence is unconditionally valid. In the *Mishna* itself diverging opinions are, very frequently, placed in juxtaposition, and the *Gemara* almost throughout takes on the nature of a lecture hall or a collection of minutes of the discussions, in which the *Amoraim* cleared up that which had been said of the *Tannaim*. Direct statements as to what is *Halacha*, valid law, are rare in the *Mishna*. Accordingly it is highly preposterous to cause all the utterances of a single rabbi found in the Talmud to stand without further ado as teaching of the Talmud, or to hold Judaism responsible for such utterances."

The *Mishna* was written in what was then Modern Hebrew, quite unlike that of the *Bible*. It is not so flowery and picturesque, but rather terse, concise and clear, suited to the legal matters with which it mainly deals.

---

* Hermann L. Strack, *Introduction to the Talmud and Midrash* (English translation), Jewish Publication Society, 1931, p. 89.

The *Gemara* is written in the main in the vernacular, a mixture of Aramaic and Hebrew, with a sprinkling of Greek, Roman and Persian words. It is marked by a disregard of grammar, and is often awkward in its lack of style, retaining always the flavor of vernacular speech. The discussions sometimes seem lengthy and pointless; occasionally they indulge in hair splitting. They may jump from subject to subject. The records appear like informal discussions, interpolated with beautiful legends, anecdotes, parables, and ethical maxims. These were often cited for the purpose of illustration, of bringing out a point, or of proving the antiquity and ancient tradition of the law discussed. Often as not, however, they had no relation to the subject under discussion, but were brought in for the sole purpose of breaking up the monotony of the lengthy discourse, and as it were, to ease the tedious study of the dry subject by something sweet and palatable. Thus the *Talmud* served as a storehouse of folklore, history, ancient custom, and wisdom, which, undoubtedly, would have otherwise disappeared, and which, next to the *Bible* itself, have preserved and helped to shape the culture and spirit and life-ways of the Jew.

*   *   *

In preparing this anthology the editor has endeavored to present the material for a first-hand acquaintance with the monumental and much discussed work, the *Babylonian Talmud*. He has thus made, as it were, a cross-section of its copious volumes.

The form and arrangement of the anthology adhere to the pattern of the *Talmud*. First the *Mishna* is cited, then follows its discussion, here kept within representative limits. The legends, stories and parables appear in the same places as in the Talmud, so that its character is here preserved. The tractates follow the original order, with one exception, that of the tractate *Aboth* (Fathers of the *Mishna*), here given in its entirety at the start. In the *Talmud* it is included within the order of *Nezikin*, which deals with law and legal procedure.

As much as possible, the style and the linguistic mannerism of the original have been preserved. The *King James* version is followed for all *Biblical* quotations, save a few where that version alters the meaning of what is being discussed in the *Talmud*.

Thanks are due to Samuel K. Mirsky, professor of Rabbinics at the Yeshiva College of New York, who read the manuscript, for his helpful counsel and advice; to Dr. Joseph T. Shipley for his stylistic suggestions; to Sylvia Loeb, who assisted in preparing the typescript, and to Ruth Busch for the checking of the proofs.

Leo Auerbach.

FATHERS OF THE MISHNA

TRACTATE ABOTH

Fathers of the Mishna

(TRACTATE ABOTH)

I

MOSES received the *Torah* (the Law) at Sinai and passed it on to Joshua, Joshua to the Elders, the Elders to the Prophets, and the Prophets passed it on to the men of the Great Assembly. They said three things: Be patient in rendering decisions; bring forth many disciples; and make a fence around the *Torah*.

Simon the Just was of the last of the Great Assembly. He used to say: The world exists because of three things: the Law, labor, and the performance of good deeds.

Antigonus, a man from Soco, received it from Simon the Just. He used to say: Be not as slaves, who serve the master for the reward that they receive, but be as the servants who wait upon the Rabbi without thought of recompense, and let the fear of the Lord be upon thee.

Yosi ben Yoezer, a man of Zeredah, and Yosi ben Yohanan, a man of Jerusalem, received it from them. They would say: Let thy house be a meeting place of scholars and let thee be covered with the dust of their feet, and imbibe their words with thirst.

Yosi ben Yohanan of Jerusalem says: Let thy house be open wide and let poor people be members of thy household. Hold not lengthy discourse with the woman: this is said of one's own woman; so much the more does it apply to the woman of another man. Therefore the sages said: All of the time that a man spends in lengthy discourse with a woman, he causes evil unto himself and idles away precious time from the study of the Law, and his end shall be that he shall inherit Hell.

Joshua ben Prahiah and Nathai the Arbelite received it from them. Joshua ben Prahiah says: Take unto thyself a teacher, and acquire a friend, and judge every person in favorable light.

Nathai the Arbelite says: Keep away from a bad neighbor and associate not with an evil man, and despair not of misfortune.

Yehuda ben Tabai and Simon ben Shetah received the Law from them. Yehuda ben Tabai says: Do not constitute thyself an advocate and when litigants appear before thee let them be in thine eyes as evil men, but when they leave let them be in thine eyes as blameless, inasmuch as they have accepted the verdict.

Simon ben Shetah says: Cross-examine the witnesses thoroughly and be cautious with thy words, because from them they may learn to speak falsely.

Shemaiah and Abtalion received it from them. Shemaiah says: Love labor, detest officialdom, and seek not the acquaintance of the authorities.

Abtalion says: Scholars, be cautious of your words for they may cause you to be exiled to a place with polluted waters and your disciples who follow you will drink of the water and die, and the name of the Lord will be profaned.

Hillel and Shamai received the Law from them. Hillel says: Be of the disciples of Aaron; love peace and pursue peace, love humanity and bring them nearer to the Law.

He would say: A man who misuses his name shall soon lose his reputation. He who does not increase his knowledge shall lose it. He who abandons learning deserves death. He who curries favor of the Crown shall vanish.

He used to say: If I be not for myself, who shall be for me; and if I am by myself what am I? and if not now—when?

Shamai says: Make of your study a permanent habit. Say little and do much, and receive every person with courtesy.

Rabban Gamaliel used to say: Appoint a teacher for thyself, and eliminate doubt.

His son Simon says: Throughout my whole life I grew up amidst scholars and have found nothing more precious than silence; nor is the speech of importance, but the deed; and he who increases words causes sin.

Rabbi Simon ben Gamaliel says: The world exists because of three things: truth, justice, and peace, as is said: (*Zechariah* viii, 16) *Execute the judgment of truth and peace in your gates.*

II

ABBI says: Which is the right road that a man should select for himself? That which is glory to its maker, and will bring honor to him from men; and be just as careful with a minor precept as with a major one, because thou knowest not the worth of a precept to reckon its loss against its worth, and the reward as against the loss. Be aware of three things and thou shalt keep away from sin: know what there is above thee;—an eye that sees, and an ear that hears, and all thy deeds are inscribed in a book.

Rabban Gamaliel, the son of Yehuda the Prince, says: The study of the *Torah* goes well with worldly occupation, for absorption in both fields keeps a man away from sin; and all learning with no menial occupation will avail a man naught and will cause him to sin. Those who occupy themselves with community affairs must do so in the name of the Lord. The glory of their fathers sustains them, and their righteousness shall endure forever. And as for you, I bestow upon you many rewards as if you yourself had accomplished it.

Be careful in your dealings with authorities—they do not befriend you unless for their own sake; they appear as friends when it suits them, but forsake one as soon as good fortune fails him.

He would say: Make the Lord's will thy will, so that He will make your wish His wish; sacrifice your will before His will so that He shall sacrifice the will of others for yours.

Hillel says: Do not stand aloof in thy community, and do not trust in thyself till the day of thy death, and do not judge thy friend until thou findest thyself in his position. Do not say a thing can not be understood which could be understood later. Say not, I shall study later when I am at leisure, because thou mayest not have the opportunity later.

He would say: A boor does not fear to commit sin; an ignorant man cannot be pious; he that is bashful shall not learn; he that is impatient cannot teach; he that is entirely taken up with trade cannot be wise; and in a place where there does not seem to be a man, endeavor thou to be a man.

He saw a skull floating upon the surface of the water and exclaimed to it: Since thou hast drowned, someone has drowned thee, and those who are responsible for thy drowning shall be drowned in turn.

He would say: He that increases his flesh, increases vermin; he that accumulates possession increases worry; he that increases his womenfolk increases witchcraft; he that increases maidservants increases whoring; he that increases slaves increases thievery; he that increases learning increases life; he that increases study increases wisdom; he that increases council increases understanding; he that increases charity increases peace; he has secured for himself a good name, he has secured for himself the teachings of the Law and has secured life in the world to come.

Rabban Yohanan ben Zakai received the Law from
Hillel and from Shamai. He used to say: If thou hast
devoted much time to learning do not pride thyself upon
it, because for that purpose thou hast been created. Rabban Yohanan ben Zakai had five disciples and they were:
Rabbi Eliezer ben Hurcanus, Rabbi Joshua ben Hananiah, Rabbi Yosi Hacohen, Rabbi Simon ben Nathaniel
and Rabbi Eleazer ben Arack. He would recount their
praise: Rabbi Eliezer ben Hurcanus is a plastered cis-
tern that loses not a drop; Rabbi Joshua ben Hananiah
brought happines: to his bearer; Rabbi Yosi is pious;
Rabbi Simon ben Nathaniel is without sin; and Rabbi
Eleazer is like a spring that gathers force. He used to say:
If one puts all the sages of Israel on one side of the scale
and Eliezer ben Hurcanus on the other side, he will outweigh them all. Aba Saul says in his name: If you put
all of the sages of Israel on one side of the scale and
Eliezer ben Hurcanus be among them, and Eleazer ben
Arack on the other side, he will outweigh them all.

He said to them: Go forth and see which is the right
road for a man to choose? Rabbi Eliezer says: A good
eye. Rabbi Joshua says: A good companion. Rabbi
Yosi says: A good neighbor. Rabbi Simon says: He that
can foresee the outcome of things. Rabbi Eleazer says:
A good heart. He answered them: I prefer the words
of Eleazer ben Arack, for his words contain all the words
of every one of you. Then he said to them: Go forth
and see which is wrong, which a man should shun?
Rabbi Eliezer says: An evil eye. Rabbi Joshua says:
A bad colleague. Rabbi Yosi says: An evil neighbor.
Rabbi Simon says: He who borrows and does not repay,
for he is as if he had borrowed from the Lord, as it

was said: (*Psalms* xxxvii, 21) *The wicked borroweth, and payeth not again; but the righteous showeth mercy and giveth.* Rabbi Eleazer says: An evil heart. He said to them: I prefer the words of Eleazer ben Arack, for his words contain all of your words.

They said three things. Rabbi Eliezer says: Let the honor of thy friend be as dear to thee as thy own. Arouse not thy anger easily. Repent a day before thou diest. Warm thyself by the light of wise men, but be cautious of their glow, lest thou be scourged; their bite is the bite of a fox; their sting is the sting of a scorpion; their hiss is the hiss of a serpent, and all their words are as burning coal.

Rabbi Joshua says: An evil eye and an evil impulse, and the hatred of mankind, put a man out of the world.

Rabbi Yosi says: Let the money of thy friend be as valuable to thee as thy own, and set thyself to learn the Law which is not thy heritage, and all thy deeds shall be for the sake of Heaven.

Rabbi Simon says: Be careful in the reading of the *Shema* (*Hear, Oh Israel*) and in thy prayers, and when thou sayest thy prayers make not thy prayer a routine, but pray with compassion and supplication before the Lord, as was said: (*Jonah* iv, 2) *Thou art a gracious God, and merciful, slow to anger, and of great kindness, and repentest thee of the evil.* And be not wicked in thine own eyes.

Rabbi Eleazer says: Be diligent in thy study of the Law, and know what to answer to the unbeliever, and know for whom thou strivest, and be confident of thy master that he will reward thee for thy effort.

Rabbi Tarphon says: The day is short, and the task

is great; the workers are lazy; the fee is large, and the master is persistent.

He would say: It is not for thee to complete the work, but neither art thou free to abandon it. If thou hast learned much of the *Torah* thou shalt be rewarded for it; thy master is sure to reward thee justly for thy work, and know that the reward of the righteous is in the future to come.

III

AKABIAH ben Mahalalel says: Consider three things before thou committest a transgression: whence cometh thou, and whither art thou going, and before Whom thou shalt give an accounting. Whence cometh thou? from a putrid drop; and where art thou going? to dust and vermin; and before Whom shalt thou give an accounting? before the King of Kings, the Holy One, blessed be He.

Rabbi Hanina the priest says: Pray for peace of the rulers, because if it were not for the fear of them, each would devour the other alive. Rabbi Hanina ben Tardion says: Two who sit without words of learning between them are as a session of scoffers, as was said: (*Psalms* i, 1) *Nor sitteth in the seat of the scoffers.* But two who sit and entertain words of the *Turah,*—the spirit of the Lord rests among them, as was said: (*Malachi* iii, 16) *Then they that feared the Lord spake often, one to the other and the Lord hearkened, and a book of remembrance was written before Him for them that feared the Lord and that thought upon His name.* Of two it is spoken, but even one who sits by himself and studies the Law, the Lord, blessed be He, designates his reward, as was said: (*Lamentations* iii, 28) *He sitteth alone and keepeth silence, because he hath borne it upon him.*

Rabbi Simon says: Three that ate at a table and spoke not the words of the Law are as if they ate of the sacrificial offerings of the death, as it was spoken: (*Isaiah* xxviii, 8) *For all the tables are full of vomit and filthiness so there is no place clean.* But three who are at one table and spoke the words of the *Torah* there, are as if they ate from the table of the Lord, as was said: (*Ezekiel* xli, 22) *And he said unto me, "This is the table that is before the Lord."*

Rabbi Haninah ben Hachinai says: He that awakens in the night, who walketh on the road alone and turns his heart to vanity, he is liable with his life.

Rabbi Nehonia ben Hachinah says: He who accepts upon himself the burdens of the Law receives exoneration from the duties of the Government and the duties of worldly care.

Rabbi Halafta from the village of Haniniah says: Ten that sit and study the *Torah,* the spirit of the Lord hovers among them, as was spoken: (*Psalms* lxxii, 1) *God standeth in the congregation of the mighty*; And even if five, as was said: (*Amos* lx, 6) *And hath founded his troops in the earth;* and even if three, as is said: (*Psalms* lxxxii, 1) *He judgeth among the gods;* and even if two, as is said: (*Malachi* iii, 16) *Then they that feared the Lord spoke often to one another and the Lord hearkened and heard it;* and even if one, as is said: (*Exodus* xx, 24) *In all places where I record my name I will come unto thee and I will bless thee.*

Rabbi Eleazar from Bartutha says: Give unto Him of His own, because thou and all thou possess are from Him; and thus spoke David: (*I Chronicles* xxix, 14) *For all things come of Thee and of Thine own have we given Thee.* Rabbi Simon says: He that walketh in the road and interrupts his study and says, "How beautiful is this tree and how beautiful are these fields," the Scriptures reckon it as if he were liable with his life.

Rabbi Dostai ben Rabbi Jana says in the name of Rabbi Meir: He that forgets one word of his studies brings upon himself the *Scriptures* as if he were guilty of his life, as is said: (*Deuteronomy* iv, 9) *Only take heed to thyself and keep thy soul diligently lest thou forget the things which thine eyes have seen.* Does this refer to one even if his study was too difficult for him? The *Scriptures* say: (*Deuteronomy* iv, 9) *Lest they depart from thy heart all the days of thy life.*

Rabbi Haninah ben Dosa says: He that puts the fear of sin above his wisdom, his wisdom will endure, but he that puts his wisdom above the fear of sin, his wisdom will not endure. He would say: He whose deeds are greater than his wisdom, his wisdom will endure, but he whose wisdom is greater than his deeds, his wisdom will not endure.

He used to say: He that gives satisfaction to men, satisfied the Lord, but he with whom mankind is not satisfied, does not satisfy the Lord. Rabbi Dosa ben Harkinus says: Morning sleep, midday wine, childish talk, and sitting in the company of ignorant men, put a man out of the world.

Rabbi Eleazar of Modeim says: He that desecrates that which is holy, that profanes the feast days and shames his fellowman in public, that breaks the covenant of our father Abraham; he that interprets the Law not in accordance with the statutes—even if he possesses

learning and good deeds—shall not have a share in the
world to come.

Rabbi Ishmael says: Be swift before a superior, be
kind to the young, and receive every person with cheer-
fulness.

Rabbi Akiba says: Laughter and light-headedness
bring a man to lewdness. Tradition is a fence around the
Law.   Taxes (Tithes) are a fence around riches, vows
are a fence around purity; a fence around wisdom is
silence.

He would say: Blessed is man because he was born in
the image of the Lord; blessed, indeed, is man because
he was born in the Image, as is said: (*Genesis* ix, 6)
For in the image of God, made he man.   Beloved are the
children of Israel because they were called children of
the Lord, as was said: (*Deuteronomy* xiv, 1) *Ye are
the children of the Lord, your God.*   A greater love is
bestowed upon them because they were favored with
a precious instrument.   It is known to them that they
were given an instrument with which the world was created.   As it is said: (*Proverbs* iv, 2) *For I give you good
doctrine, forsake ye not My law.*

All is foreseen but freedom of choice is granted, and
the world is judged with charity and all is measured by
the number of good deeds.

He would say: All is given against a pledge and a net
is spread over all living, and the shop is open, and the
storekeeper allows credit, and the ledger is open, and the
hand inscribes, and whosoever wants credit shall come
and borrow.   But the collectors make their rounds regu-
larly each day and exact payment from each man whether
he is aware of it or not, and they have the things on

which to rely, and the judgment is a true judgment, and everything is ready for the banquet.

Rabbi Eleazar ben Azariah says: If there is no learning, there is no good breeding. If there is no good breeding, there is no learning. If there is no wisdom, there is no fear. If there is no fear, there is no wisdom. If there is no understanding, there is no knowledge. If there is no knowledge, there is no understanding. If there is no bread, there is no learning; and if there is no learning, there is no bread. He used to say: He whose wisdom is in excess of his deeds is likened to the tree whose branches are many and its roots are few. A wind comes and uproots it and turns it over, as is said: (*Jeremiah* xvii, 6) *For he shall be like the heat in the desert, and shall not see when good cometh; but shall inhabit the parched places in the wilderness, and in a salt land and not inhabited.* But he whose deeds are in excess of his wisdom is like a tree whose branches are few but its roots are many. Though all the winds of the world may come and blow at it, they shall not stir it from its place, as is said: (*Jeremiah* xvii, 8) *For he shall be as a tree planted by the waters, and that spreadeth out her roots by the river, and shall not see when heat cometh, but her leaf shall be green and shall not be careful in the year of draught, neither shall cease from yielding fruit.*

Rabbi Eliezer ben Hisma says: Nests, and the onset of menstruation: those are the essentials of law; calculations of the calendar and geometry are the sweetmeats of wisdom.

IV

BEN Zoma says: Who is wise? He who learns from every man, as was said: (*Psalms* cxix, 99) *I am learned beyond any of my teachers.* Who is mighty? He who can master his passions, as was said: (*Proverbs* xvi, 32) *He that is slow to anger is better than the mighty and he that ruleth his spirit than he that taketh a city.* Who is rich? He that is happy with his portion, as was said: (*Psalms* cxxviii, 2) *For thou shalt eat the labor of thine hands, happy shalt thou be, and it shall be well with thee.* Happy in this world and happy in the world to come. Who is honored? He that honors his fellowman, as was said: (*I Samuel* ii, 30) *For them that honor Me, I will honor, and they that despise Me shall be lightly esteemed.*

Ben Azzai says: Run to fulfill a minor precept as if it were a major precept, and run away from transgression, for a precept draws another precept, and a transgression draws another transgression. The reward of a precept is another precept, and the reward of a transgression is another transgression.

He used to say: Despise no one and discriminate not against a thing; for there is not a man but has his hour, and there is not a thing but has its place.

Rabbi Levitas of Yabne says: Be lowly in spirit, for the expectation of a man is but the worm. Rabbi Yo-

hanan ben Berocca says: Whosoever profanes the name
of God in secret, shall have the penalty exacted from him
in public. Whether one errs, or whether one profanes
deliberately.

Rabbi Ishmael says: He who learns in order to teach
is given the opportunity to learn and to teach. He who
learns in order to practice is given the opportunity to
learn, to teach, to observe and to practice.

Rabbi Zaddok says: Make not thy learning a crown
wherewith to boast of thyself, and make it not a spade
wherewith to dig, for Hillel used to say: He who maketh
use of the crown shall vanish. Thou mayest know that
he that benefits from his learning removes his life from
the world.

Rabbi Yosi says: He that honors the *Torah* is honored by mankind. He that profanes the *Torah* shall be
scorned by mankind.

His son, Rabbi Ishmael says: He who refrains from
passing judgments avoids enmity, robbery and false
swearing; and he who is ill-mannered is a fool, wicked
and haughty.

He used to say: Pass not judgment by yourself;
there is only One who may; and say not: Accept my
opinion; for they may do it, but not thee.

Rabbi Jonathan says: Whosoever fulfills the *Torah*
in poverty, shall finally fulfill it in riches; and whosoever
neglects the *Torah* in riches shall finally neglect it in poverty.

Rabbi Meir says: Occupy thyself less with trade, and
devote thyself to the *Torah*. Be meek before all men.
If thou hast neglected the Law many things shall be

neglected for thee, but if thou hast labored for the *Torah,* many rewards are in store for thee.

Rabbi Eliezer ben Jacob says: Whosoever fulfills one precept secures for himself one defender. Whosoever commits one transgression secures for himself one accuser. Repentence and good deeds are a shield against misfortune.

Rabbi Yohanan, the shoemaker, says: A society that has been consecrated in the name of the Lord shall endure, but a society that is not consecrated in the name of the Lord shall not endure.

Rabbi Eleazar ben Shamua says: Let the honor of thy disciple be as dear to thee as thine honor, and the honor of thy colleague as respected as thy teacher's, and the honor of thy teacher's as respected as the honor of the Lord.

Rabbi Yehuda says: Be careful in thy studies, for errors in study cause presumptuousness.

Rabbi Simon says: There are three crowns: the crown of the *Torah,* the crown of priesthood, and the crown of kingdom; but the crown of a good name is greater than any of them.

Rabbi Nehorai says: Exile thyself to a place of learning and say not that the *Torah* will follow thee, that thy colleagues will establish it for thee; and rely not on thine own judgment.

Rabbi Yanai says: It is not in our power to explain the security of the wicked, nor the suffering of the righteous.

Rabbi Mathia ben Heresh says: Be first to greet every man; and be a tail unto the lion, and be not a head to the fox.

Rabbi Jacob says: This world is like a vestibule before the world to come. Prepare thyself in the vestibule, so that thou mayest enter the banquet hall.

He would say: One hour of repentence and good deeds in this world is worth more than all life in the world to come; and better is one hour of contentment in the world to come than all life in this world.

Rabbi Simeon ben Eleazer says: Pacify not thy friend in the moment of his anger, and comfort him not while his deceased lies before him; question him not while he is making his vow, and endeavor not to see him at the moment of his disgrace.

Samuel the Younger says: (*Prov.* xxiv, 17) *Rejoice not when thine enemy falleth, and let not thine heart be glad when he stumbleth: Lest the Lord see it, and it displease him and he turn away his wrath from him.*

Elisha ben Abuyah says: He that learns as a child is like ink written on new paper, he that learns while he is old is like ink written on a blotted paper.

Rabbi Yosl bar Yehuda from Kfar-Babli says: He who learns from the young is like one who eats unripe grapes and drinks wine out of the wine press. He who learns from the old is like one who eats ripe grapes and drinks old wine. The Rabbi says: Look not at the jug but at what it contains. There may be a new jug that containeth old wine, and an old jug that containeth not even new wine.

Rabbi Eleazar Hakappar says: Envy, lust and ambition put a man out of the world.

He used to say: Those who were born are to die, and those who are dead are to be born again; those who are alive are to be judged, to know, to proclaim, and to

make known that He is the Lord, the Master, the Creator;
He, the Discerner; He, the Judge; He, the Witness; He,
the Complainant; and He shall surely judge. Blessed
be He. Before Him there is no injustice and no forget-
ting, nor regard for persons, nor taking of bribes, for all
is His, and everything will accord with the reckoning.
And let thy impulse not assure thee that the grave is thy
refuge, for without thy will hast thou been created, and
despite thy will art thou alive and despite thy will shalt
thou die, and despite thy will art thou bound to give a
reckoning before the King of Kings, the Holy One.
Blessed be He.

V

ITH ten maxims was the world created. The learned may say: It could have been created with one. This was done in order to punish the wicked who destroy this world that was created with ten maxims, and to give many rewards to the just who sustain this world that was created with ten maxims. There were ten generations from Adam to Noah; to show how patient the Lord is. So many generations had vexed Him till He brought upon them the deluge. There are ten generations from Noah to Father Abraham; to show how patient the Lord is, for ten generations had vexed Him till Father Abraham appeared and received the reward of all of them. Ten times was Father Abraham tried, and came through each time to show how great was the love of the Lord in Abraham. Ten miracles were performed to our fathers in Egypt and ten at the sea. Ten plagues were brought upon the Egyptians and ten at the sea. Ten times have our fathers tempted the Lord in the desert, as was said: (*Numbers* xiv, 22) *And ye have tempted me now these ten times, and have not hearkened to my voice.* Ten miracles have been performed for our fathers in the temple. No woman has miscarried because of the odor of the sacred flesh, and the sacred flesh never became putrid, and never was a fly seen in the slaughter house, and never has pollution come upon the High Priest

on the day of Atonement, and the rains have not extin-
guishd the fires of the fuel pile, and no wind has pre-
vailed against the pillar of smoke, no defect was found
in the *Omer* or in the two loaves of bread. People stood
together yet prostrated themselves in comfort. And no
snake or scorpion ever stung anyone in Jerusalem, and
no man ever said to his fellow: (*Isaiah* xlix, 20) *I cannot find lodging in Jerusalem.* Ten things were created
at twilight on the eve of the Sabbath: the mouth of the
earth, the mouth of the well, the mouth of the she-ass,
the rainbow, manna, the rod of Moses, the diamond, letters, and writing, and the Tablets. Some say also the
evil spirits and the grave of Moses, and the ram of Abraham, our father.

Some say also, the tongs made with tongs.

There are seven types of fool and seven of wise man.
A wise man does not speak before one who is greater
than he in wisdom and in years, does not interrupt the
conversation of his fellows. He is not hasty with his
answers, inquires what is pertinent, and answers in accordance with the Law, speaks of the first subject first,
and of the last, last. If he does not know, he says: I
know it not, and accepts the truth. The opposite are the
characteristics of the fool.

Seven kinds of punishments are meted out to the
world for seven kinds of transgressions. If some give
the tithe, and others do not give it, there comes a famine
from drought; some go hungry and some have plenty.
When all decide not to give the tithe, a famine, the result
of chaos and drought, comes upon the world. If the people set not apart the offering of dough, there comes the
famine of extermination.

Pestilence comes upon the world for capital crimes mentioned in the *Torah,* that are not referred to the court, and for not letting the ground lie fallow in the seventh year.

The sword comes upon the world when justice is suppressed or perverted. And because of them who teach the *Torah* not in accordance with the Law. Wild beasts come upon the world because of false swearing and the profanation of the name of the Lord. Exile comes upon the world because of idolatry, for incest, for bloodshed, and for not letting the land lie fallow in the sabbatical year.

At four periods does pestilence increase; at the fourth year, at the beginning and at the end of the seventh, and at the ending of the Fast of Tabernacles each year. At the fourth year, because of the tithe for the poor that is due in the third year. At the seventh because of the tithe for the poor due in the sixth. At the end of the seventh because of the produce from the fields that should have lain fallow. At the conclusion of the Fast because of the stealing of the gifts for the poor.

There are four types of men. The one that says: Mine is mine and thine is thine; this is the common type. And some say this is the attitude of Sodom. The one that says: Mine is thine and thine is mine; this is the ignorant. Mine is thine and thine is thine:—a pious man. Mine is mine and thine is mine; this is the attitude of the wicked.

There are four types of temperament. Quick in anger, and as soon appeased. His gain is voided by his loss. Slow to anger but hard to appease. His loss is voided by his gain. Slow to anger but easy to appease. He is kindly. Quick to anger but hard to appease. He is wicked.

There are four types of students. Quick to absorb and quick to forget. His gain is voided by his loss. Slow to absorb and slow to forget. His loss is voided by his gain. Quick to absorb and slow to forget. He is smart. Slow to absorb but quick to forget. This is bad.

There are four ways of giving charity. One wishes to give but wants no one else to give. This is unjust towards others. One wishes others to give but himself refuses. This is evil on his part. One gives and wishes others to give. He is pious. One will not give and wants no one else to. He is wicked.

There are four types who enroll in the House of Study. He that attends but does nothing. He gets the benefit of attendance. He that studies but does not attend. The reward of study is his portion. Attends and studies—he is pious. Attends not and studies not—he is wicked.

There are four types who sit at the feet of the sages; a sponge, a funnel, a strainer and a sieve. The sponge absorbs everything indiscriminately. The funnel takes in at one end and lets out at the other. The strainer lets through the wine and retains the lees. The sieve lets off the bran and retains the flour.

All love based on ulterior motives will cease when the motives cease. But love that depended not on ulterior motives will never cease. Love that is based on ulterior motives is as the love of Amnon and Tamar. Love that is not based on ulterior motives is as the love of David and Jonathan.

A controversy that is for the sake of the Lord will at the end bring forth something of permanent value. A controversy that is not for the sake of the Lord shall come to naught. What is a controversy for the sake of the Lord? The controversy of Hillel and Shamai. And what is not for the sake of the Lord? That is the controversy of Korah and all of his congregation.

Whosoever bestirs others to do the right, shall himself never cause sin. Whosoever leads others to commit sin, shall himself never find repentance. Moses was righteous and bestirred others to do right. The righteousness of others was added to his account, as was said: (*Deuteronomy* xxxiii, 21) *He executed the justice of the Lord, and his judgment with Israel.* Jeroboam sinned and led others to sin. The sin of others is accredited to him, as was said: (1 *Kings* xv, 30) *Because of the sins of Jeroboam, which he sinned, and which he made Israel sin.*

Whosoever possesses three certain things, is of the disciples of our father, Abraham; whosoever, three other things, is of the disciples of Balaam, the wicked. A benevolent eye, a meek spirit, and a humble heart—is of the disciples of Father Abraham. A wicked eye, a bold spirit, and a proud heart is of the disciples of Balaam, the wicked. What is the difference between the disciples of Father Abraham and the disciples of Balaam, the wicked? The disciples of Father Abraham benefit in this world and shall inherit the world to come, as was said: (*Proverbs* viii, 21) *That I may cause those that love me to inherit substance; and I will fill their treasures.* But the disciples of Balaam shall inherit Hell and go down to the depths of desolation, as was said:

(Psalms ii, 23) *But Thou, O God, shalt bring them down into the pit of destruction: bloody and deceitful men shall not live out half their days; but I will trust in Thee.*

Yehuda ben Tema says: Be as fierce as the panther, lightwinged as the eagle, swift as the deer and strong as the lion, to do the bidding of thy Father in Heaven.

He used to say: The insolent shall go to Hell and the modest to Heaven. Lord, our God, may it be Thy will to build our City soon in our days, and let our lot be Thy *Torah.*

He would say: Age of five is for reading, ten for *Mishna,* thirteen for precepts, fifteen for *Talmud,* eighteen for marriage, twenty for pursuits, thirty for strength, forty for wisdom, fifty for council, sixty of ripe age, eighty of power, ninety of decline. A man of one hundred is as dead and gone out of this world.

Ben Bag-Bag says: Turn the Law this way and that way, everything can be found therein. Thou shalt get old and gray, but turn not away from the *Torah.* There is no better rule for thee.

Ben He-He says: The reward is commensurate with the effort.

AGRICULTURE

ZERAIM

The Portion of the Poor

(TRACTATE PEAH)

THE following have no prescribed measure: *Peah,** First-Fruits, Festival-Offerings, deeds of kindness, and the study of the Law. And the following are the things the fruit of which a man enjoys in this world, but the capital fund of which remains for him in the world to come: The honoring of father and mother, deeds of kindness, and the making of peace between one man and another, but the study of the Law is greater than any of them.

One should not leave *Peah* less than one-sixth of the field. And although there is no prescribed measure it should be fixed according to the size of the field, the number of the poor, and the need.

One may leave *Peah* in the beginning or in the middle of the field. Rabbi Simon says: As long as he leaves at the end the prescribed measure. Rabbi Yehuda says:

---

* Peah: corner of the field, the portion of the crop that must be left by the owner to the poor. See *Leviticus* xix, 9, xxiii, 22.

If he leaves but one stalk at the end, he has fulfilled his obligation as to *Peah*; but if not, whatever he left at the beginning or at the end is regarded as abandoned property.

A ruling has been established as regards *Peah*: whatever is used as food, and has to be tended, and is raised from the soil, and is reaped at one time, and is brought in for storage, requires the leaving of *Peah*; and this includes grain and pulse.

Of the trees, sumach, carob, nut trees, the almond, vines, the pomegranate, the olive, and date palm are all subject to *Peah*.

THE following serve as boundaries for a field, in all that concerns *Peah*: A river, a pond, a private road, a public road, and a public path. Also a private path that is used during the summer and during the rainy-season, uncultivated soil, fallow-land, and a different variety of crop. If one cuts the produce of one field for fodder, he makes thereby a boundary, this is according to Rabbi Meir, but the Sages say: It does not act as a boundary unless he ploughed it up.

A stream, both sides of which cannot be cut in one operation serves as a boundary, according to Rabbi Yehuda. The hills that can be ploughed by a mattock, though the oxen cannot go through them with their plough, is considered one field, and is subject to only one *Peah*.

Everything serves as a boundary for a sown field, but for trees a fence only serves as a boundary, but if the branches of the trees intertwine, then the fence does not constitute a boundary, and all is subject to only one *Peah*.

FROM CHAPTER I

PEAH is given from what is attached to the soil. From vines and date palms, the owner takes down some fruit and distributes it to the poor. Rabbi Simon says: This applies also to nut trees.

If ninety-nine of the poor vote that *Peah* be distributed, and one says that it should be left for them to help themselves, it is to be done according to the one because the law is in agreement with him.

But it is not so with vines and date palms; if ninety-nine vote for helping themselves and one says it should be distributed, he is followed, because the law is in agreement with him.

If one took some of the *Peah* and threw it over the rest, none of it belongs to him. If he fell upon it or spread his cloak over it, it must be taken away from him. The same applies to Gleaning and to Forgotten Sheaf.

Peah must not be cut with a sickle and must not be uprooted with a hatchet, so that one will not hurt his neighbor.

If a heathen reaped his field and then became a proselyte, he is exempt from Gleaning, from Forgotten Sheaf, and from *Peah*. Rabbi Yehuda says: He is subject to the Forgotten Sheaf, because this is given at the time of binding.

What constitutes Gleaning? Whatever falls down at the time of reaping. If one cut a handful, or pulled up a handful, and a thorn pricked him and it fell from his hands to the ground, it belongs to the owner. If it fell on the inside of the hand or the inside of the sickle, it be-

longs to the poor; if it fell on the outside of the hand or
the back of the sickle, it belongs to the owner. If it fell
over the top of the hand or the top of the sickle, Rabbi
Ishmael says: It belongs to the poor. Rabbi Akiba says:
It belongs to the owner.   FROM CHAPTER II

FROM a stack of sheaves beneath which no Gleaning has been taken, everything that touches the ground
belongs to the poor. If the wind scattered the sheaves
from the stack, one must estimate the amount of gleanings that would be gathered from the field and give it to
the poor. Rabbi Simon ben Gamaliel says: One gives in
proportion to the yield of the field.

If a man sells a field the seller may take the gleanings,
but the buyer must not take any. One must not hire
workers with the stipulation that the worker's son shall
gather the gleanings behind him. One who does not allow the poor to gather, or allows one, and does not allow
another; or if he aids one of them, he is robbing the poor.
Of such a one it was said: (*Proverbs* xxii, 28) *Remove
not the ancient landmark which thy fathers have set.* (The
Mishna reads the word "Olam" as "Olim" and trans-
lates the second part of the verse: for those that come
up.)   FROM CHAPTER VII

A POOR man who goes from one place to another
should be given not less than a loaf worth one *Pandion,*
and one *Selah's* worth of grain. If he stays for the
night, he should be given his needs for the night. On the
Sabbath he should be given three meals.

If a man has food for two meals, he should not take
any food from the public kitchen. If he has food enough

for fourteen meals, he should not take anything from the charity chest. Money for the charity chest is to be collected by two, and should be distributed by three.

If a man has two hundred *Zuz,* he must not take Gleanings, Forgotten-Sheaf, *Peah,* and Poor-man's Tithe. But if he has two hundred less one *Denar,* even if a thousand was given to him at one time, he may still take everything that is allowed to a poor man. If his money is pledged to a debtor, or for his wife's marriage contract, he may take of the poor man's portions. A man must not be compelled to sell his house or his tools.

If one has fifty *Zuz,* and he trades with them, he must not take of the poor man's portions. He who does not need and takes will not die of old age, until he has been compelled to seek the aid of his fellow man. But one who needs and does not take any, will not die of old age, till he shall be in a position to aid others. Of him it was said: (*Jeremiah* xvii, 7) *Blessed is the man that trusteth in the Lord, and whose hope the Lord is.* And this applies also to the judge who renders a true verdict according to the evidence. And every person who is not lame, blind or dumb, but pretends that he is; shall not die of old age before he does become like one of them, for it was said: (*Proverbs* xi, 27) *He that seeketh mischief, it shall come unto him.* And it was also said: (*Deuteronomy* xvi, 20) *That which is altogether just shalt thou follow.* A judge who accepts a bribe and perverts a decision shall not die from old age until his eyes have become blinded, for it was said: (*Exodus* xxiii, 8) *And thou shalt take no gift, for the gift blindeth the wise, and perverteth the words of the righteous.* FROM CHAPTER VIII

HOLY DAYS

MOED

Sabbath

ONE does not sit down before the barber, close to the time of the afternoon prayer, unless he has already said his prayer. Neither shall he enter the bath house or a tannery, or sit down to eat or begin a law suit; but if they have begun it, they need not interrupt it. One interrupts for the reading of "Hear, O Israel", but not for the prayer.

A tailor should not take his needle on Sabbath eve just before nightfall; he may forget and go out with it. Nor the scribe take his pen. One should not begin to clean his clothes, and one does not read at the lamplight (because he may tilt it). But the schoolmaster may supervise the reading of the children, but he himself should not read.

Similarly a man that is in heat should not eat together with a woman that is in heat, because it may lead them to sin.   (*Mishna*)

AFTER all we speak here of the usual haircut. Why
may not one sit down at the beginning? Because the
shears may be broken. Thus one may not enter the
bathhouse if only for sweating. Why not at the outset?
Because one may faint. Nor a tannery if only to inspect
it. Why not at the outset? Because one may notice
that his goods are being spoiled, and that will worry him;
nor sit down to eat, not even a small meal. Why not in
the first place? Because one may prolong the meal. Nor
to a law suit, even if at the end of it. Why not in the
first place? Because he may find a new plea for chang-
ing the decision.

What constitutes the beginning of haircutting? Rabbi Abim says: When the sheet is spread on one's knee.
What constitutes the beginning of a bath? Rabbi Abim
says: When one takes off his coat. And what is the
beginning of tanning? When one tied his apron round
his shoulders. When does the meal begin? Rabbi says:
When one washed his hands. Rabbi Hanina says: When
one loosened his girdle. There is no disagreement here.
One speaks of the Babylonians and the other of the
Palestinians.

SAID the Holy One, blessed be He, to Moses: I
have a precious gift in my treasure and its name is
"Sabbath" and I wish to give it to Israel. Go and inform them of it. From this remark I infer, said Rabbi
Simon ben Gamaliel, that if one gives a piece of bread to
a child, he must inform the mother of it. How does
one do it? He dabs him with oil and paints him with
Kohl. But how about these days, when we are afraid
of witchcraft? Rab Pupa says: One does the same.

But it is not so. For Rabbi Hama ben Rabbi Hanina says: If one makes a gift to his neighbor one does not have to inform him for it was said: (*Exodus* xxxiv, 29) *Moses wist not that the skin of his face shone while he talked with him.* There is no contradiction here. In one instance, the fact will be evident in any case. In the other instance it may not be known. The Sabbath, too, was bound to be known. But its reward was not bound to be known.

Raba ben Mehasia said, in the name of Rabbi Hama ben Goria, in the name of Raba: One should never single out one of his children. Because Jacob gave Joseph two *Selah* weight more of silk than to his other children, Joseph's brothers became jealous of him, and this finally caused our forefathers to go to Egypt.

Raba ben Mahasia, also, said in the name of Rabbi Hama ben Goria in the name of Rab: Any city whose roofs are higher than the Prayer House, will, at the end, be destroyed. As it was said: (*Ezra* ix, 9) *To set up the house of our God to repair the desolation thereof.* This refers only to regular houses, but towers and turrets are different. Rabbi Ashi said: I saw to it that the city of Mehasia was not destroyed. How so? But indeed it was destroyed. Well, it was not destroyed because of that sin.

Said Raba ben Mehasia, in the name of Rabbi bar Goria in the name of Rab: One should rather be subjected to an Ishmaelite than to a foreigner; under a stranger but not under a Parsee; under a Parsee, but not under a scholar; under a scholar but not under an orphan or a widow.

Rabbi ben Mehasia, also, said in the name of Rabbi Hama bar Goria in the name of Rab: Any sickness but not that of the bowels; any pain but not that of the heart; any ache but not that of the head; anything evil, but not an evil wife.

Rabbi bar Mehasia, also, said in the name of Rabbi Hama ben Goria in the name of Rab: If all the seas were ink and all the reeds were pens, and all the skies were parchment, and all men could write, they would not suffice to write down all the red tape of government. What in the *Scriptures* refers to this? Rabbi Meshershia said: (*Proverbs* xxv, 3) *The heaven for height, the earth for depth, and the heart of Kings is unsearchable.*

RABBI Simon ben Eleazer said in the name of Rabbi Simon ben Gamaliel: One does not arrange for the betrothal of children; one does not engage a teacher for his son, nor does he make arrangements to teach him a trade; one does not comfort mourners, nor does one visit sick people on the Sabbath. This is according to the House of Shamai, but the house of Hillel permits it.

The Rabbis taught: When one visits a sick person on the Sabbath, he says: It is Sabbath; tears are forbidden. A speedy recovery. Rabbi Meir says: One may have compassion. Rabbi Yehuda says: The Lord may have mercy on you and on the sick in Israel. Rabbi Yosi says: May the Lord have mercy on you among the sick of Israel. Shebna, a man of Jerusalem, said upon entering: Peace, and upon departing, he said: Sabbath. Tears are forbidden. A speedy recovery. His mercy is abundant; rest in peace.   (*Gemara*)

THE House of Shamai says: Ink, dyes and vetches must not be soaked on Sabbath eve, unless there is time for them to be thoroughly soaked before the Sabbath sets in. But the House of Hillel permit it. The House of Shamai says: Nets and traps must not be set to catch fish or birds or animals, unless they will be caught before sundown. But the House of Hillel permit it.

The House of Shamai says: One must not sell anything to a Gentile or help him load his beast, or put a burden on his shoulder, unless he can reach a nearby place soon, before sundown. But the House of Hillel permit it.

The House of Shamai says: Hides must not be given to a tanner, nor clothes to a Gentile launderer, unless they can be done on Sabbath eve before sundown. But the House of Hillel permit it.

Rabbi Simon ben Gamaliel said: In my father's house they used to give the linen to a Gentile launderer three days before the Sabbath. Both houses agree, however, that one may set the beams of the oil press and the rollers of the wine press.

One must not put bread in the oven on Sabbath eve before darkness, nor may cakes be put on the coal unless there is time for the crust to form. Rabbi Eliezer says: In time for the crust to form on the bottom. But the Passover offering may be put in the oven just before darkness. One may, also, kindle the fire in the chamber of the hearth, but in the country only if most of it will catch fire before darkness. Rabbi Yehuda says: If one burns coal, if any amount at all will catch fire, it is well.

(Mishna)

THE Rabbis taught: One may open a water canal into the garden on Sabbath eve, so that the water will flow all day. One may put a perfumed sachet under the clothing on Sabbath eve so that it will penetrate the clothing all day. One may put sulphur under utensils on Sabbath eve so that the process of sulphuring will go on all day. One may put a salve on the eye, a plaster on a wound so that the healing goes on all day. But one must not put more wheat in the water mill than can be ground before sundown. What is the reason?

Said Rabba: Because of the noise that it makes. Rabbi Joseph said to him: May not the Master say: Because the utensils have to rest too? For we were taught: (*Exodus* xxiii, 13) *And in all things that I have said unto you be circumspect.* That means, also, the resting of the utensils. Rabbi Joseph said: You may say: On account of the resting of the utensils.

The Rabbis taught: The House of Shamai says: One must not sell anything to a Gentile, nor lend him money, nor make a loan to him of anything, nor make a gift of it, unless he can get with it to his house before sundown. The House of Hillel says: If he can reach a house near the city wall, it is permitted. Rabbi Akiba says: As long as he can leave the house of the Jew before sundown. Said Rabbi Yosi ben Rabbi Yehuda: The words of Rabbi Akiba are the same as the words of the House of Hillel. Rabbi Akiba came only to amplify the words of the House of Hillel.

The Rabbis taught: A man must not sell his leaven bread to a non-Jew, unless he knows that the Gentile will eat it before the Passover. This is the opinion of the

House of Shamai, but the House of Hillel says: As long as the Jew may eat it, he may sell it.

The Rabbis taught: A man must not rent his utensils to a non-Jew on Sabbath eve. However, on the fourth and fifth day of the week he may do it. One does not send a letter to a Gentile on Sabbath eve, but one sends it on the fourth or fifth day of the week.

The Rabbis taught: One must not send a letter through a Gentile on Sabbath eve, though one has arranged to pay him for it, unless he can reach the house before sundown. This is according to the House of Shamai. The House of Hillel, however, says: If he can reach a house near the city wall, it is permitted. But isn't the messenger getting paid for it? Rabbi Shesheth says: This is the meaning: He must have time to reach the house. According to the House of Shamai; or according to the House of Hillel, he must reach a house near the city wall. But we learned in the first place, that one does not send at all. There is no contradiction here. One speaks of a town where there is a Post Office and the other speaks of a town where there is no Post Office.

The Rabbis taught: One must not ship on a boat less than three days before Sabbath. This refers to a pleasure trip. But if the voyage is undertaken for a good deed, it is permissible, and one should stipulate that the ship will rest on the Sabbath; but if it does not rest, it is well. Thus the word of Rabbi. Rabbi Simon ben Gamaliel says: It is not necessary. A trip from Tyre to Sidon is permitted even on Sabbath eve.

The Rabbis taught: One must not besiege a city less than three days before Sabbath, but if the siege has begun, it is not necessary to stop. And thus did Shamai say: (*Deuteronomy* xx, 20) *Until it be subdued even on the Sabbath day.*

Said Rabbi Zadok:Thus was it customary in the House of Rabbi Gamaliel. The white garments were given to the launderer three days before the Sabbath, but colored garments even on Sabbath eve. And from this we learn that white garments are harder to launder than colored garments.

Abaya said: When one gives a garment to a launderer he should give it to him by measure and take it back by measure. If he finds it larger the launderer spoiled it by stretching. If he found it smaller, he spoiled it by shrinking.   (*Gemara*)

FROM CHAPTER I

WHAT may one use for lighting on the Sabbath, and what must one not use? One must not use cedar fibre, nor oakum, nor silk, nor a bast wick, nor a desert wick, nor seaweed, nor pitch, nor wax, nor castor oil, nor burnt oil, nor tail fat, nor tallow. Nahum the Mede says: One may use boiled tallow, but the Sages say: Whether boiled or not one may not light with it.

One does not light on festival days with sanctified oil that has been defiled. Rabbi Ishmael says: One must not light with tar because of the respect for Sabbath. The Sages permit all oils: Sesame oil, nut oil, radish oil; cucumber oil, tar and Naptha. Rabbi Tarfon says: Only olive oil may be used for lighting.   (*Mishna*)

THE Rabbis taught: All the things that we were told are not to be used for lighting on the Sabbath, one may

use them to make a large fire to warm oneself by, or
to use for light, whether it is used on the hearth or in
the stove. It was only forbidden to make a wick of it,
nothing else.

Rabbi Huna said: All wicks and oils which are forbidden to be used on the Sabbath are, also, forbidden to
be used on Hanukah whether on the Sabbath or on a
weekday.

The Rabbis taught: The precept of Hanukah de-
mands a light for each man and his house. The zealous
light a candle for each one. And the very zealous? The
House of Shemai says: They light eight candles the first
day and one candle less each day. The House of Hillel
says: The first day they light one candle and each day
they add one.

Said Raba ben Bar Hanai, in the name of Rabbi
Yahanan: There were two Elders in Sidon, one acted
according to the House of Shamai, and one acted as the
House of Hillel. The first gave his reason that it should
correspond to the offerings of the festival. While the
other said: One progresses in Holy things but one does
not retrogress.

The Rabbis taught: It is decreed that the Hanukah
light be placed near the door on the outside, but if one
lives in an upper story one puts it at the window nearest
the street. But if there is danger one may put it on a
table. Raba said: An additional candle is needed if it is
to be used for light.

What is Hanukah? The Rabbis taught: On the
twenty-eighth day of Kislev begins the festival of Hanukah. It lasts eight days. On these, no lamentations for

the dead nor fasting is allowed. For when the Greeks entered the Temple they defiled all the oils. When the Hashmoneans overpowered and defeated them, they searched and found only one vial of oil which was lying with the seal of the High Priest, and there was not more in it than enough for one day, but a miracle was performed, for it burned eight days. The following year these days were decreed a festival with rejoicing, Hallelujah and thanksgiving.

It was taught: If a spark from the anvil caused a damage, the smith is liable for it. If a camel laden with flax passed through the street and some of the flax got into a store and was ignited by the storekeeper's lamp and burned the building, the camel driver is liable for the damage. But if the storekeeper put the lamp on the outside, then the storekeeper is liable.

Rabbi Yehuda says: If it were a Hanukah light, he is not liable. Rabbina said in the name of Rab: This shows that a Hanukah lamp must be put ten feet from the ground. If you think it should be more than ten, then he could have said: He should put it higher than the camel and its driver. Yet, if we put one to too much trouble, he may not observe the precept altogether.

Rabbi Kahana said: Rabbi Nathan bar Minyomi explained in Rabbi Tanhum's name: A Hanukah lamp that is put higher than twenty ells is unfit, the same as a Sukah or a marquee over an entrance.

Said Rabbi Yehuda in the name of Rabbi Ashi in the name of Rab: One must not count money by the light of a Hanukah lamp. When I said this before Samuel, he answered: Is there any sanctity attached to the lamp?

RABBI Joshua ben Levi was asked: May one make
use of the decorations of the *Sukah* during the seven
days of festival? He answered: Indeed, we were told
that one must not count money at the light of the Hanukah lamp. Said Rabbi Joseph: Lord of Abraham! he
makes what was taught hinge upon what was not taught.
As for the *Sukah,* we were explicitly taught, while as for
Hanukah, it was not taught. It was taught: If the roof
is according to the law, decorate it with hangings and
rugs and suspend from it nuts, peaches, almonds, pome-
granates, grape-clusters, garlands of ears of corn, wines,
oils and flowers. It is forbidden to use them before the
festival. But if one made a condition, all is in accordance with the condition.

RABBI Joshua ben Levi said: All the oils are fit to
be used for a lamp, but olive oil is the best. Abaya said:
At first the Master used to search for the sesame oil.
He would say that the light lasts longer, but when he
heard of what Rabbi Joshua ben Levi taught, he looked
only for olive oil. This, he said, gives a clearer light.

Rabbi Joshua ben Levi, also, said: All oils are good
for ink, but the best is olive oil. Someone asked him:
For kneading or for smoking? Come and hear: Rabbi
Samuel ben Zutra discoursed: All oils are good for ink,
but olive oil is the best, also for kneading and for smoking. Rabbi Samuel ben Zutra taught as follows: All
soots are good for ink, but olive oil is the best. Rabbi
Huna said: All resins are good for ink, but balsam resin
is the best.   (*Gemara*)

IF A man puts out the light because he is afraid of a stranger, or robbers, or an evil spirit, or because of a sick person who cannot sleep; he is exonerated. But if he puts it out because he wants to save the oil or the wick, he is guilty of transgression. Rabbi Yosi exonerates him in every case, except if he does it to save the wick, because he makes charcoal.   (*Mishna*)

SAID Rabbi Yehuda, son of Rabbi Samuel ben Shilath in the name of Rab: The sages wished to hide the book of *Ecclesiastes,* because the words of it contradicted one another. But why didn't they hide it? Because in its beginning are the words of the *Torah* and in its end are the words of the *Torah.* In the beginning come the words of the *Torah,* because it is written: (*Ecclesiastes* i, 3) *What profit hath a man of all his labor which he taketh under the sun?* And in the school of Rabbi Yanai they said: Under the sun he has none, but above the sun, he has it. And at the end come words of divine teaching. For it is written: (*Ecclesiastes* xii, 13) *Let us hear the conclusion of the whole matter. Fear God and keep his commandments for this is the whole duty of man.* Which are the words that contradict one another? It was written: (*Ecclesiastes* vii, 3) *Sorrow is better than laughter,* and it is written: (*Ecclesiastes* viii, 15) *Then I commanded mirth* and it is written: (*Ecclesiastes* ii, 2) *and of mirth, what doeth it?*

There is no difficulty here. *Sorrow is better than laughter.* This is the sorrow that the Lord expresses for the righteous in this world, which is better than the laughter that he laughs over the evil in this world. *And of laughter I said, (ibid.)* which is to be praised, refers to the laughter the Lord, blessed be He, will enjoy with the righteous in the world to come. *Then I commanded mirth* refers to the mirth that ensues from the performance of a precept. *And of mirth, what doeth it?* Refers to mirth that is not the result of a precept, to teach you that the *Shekinah* does not rest upon sorrow, nor indolence, nor frivolity, nor gossip, nor triviality, nor joy, as it was said: (*II Kings* iii, 15) *But now bring me a minstrel. And it came to pass, when the minstrel played, that the hand of the Lord came upon him.*

And the book of *Proverbs,* too, they wished to hide because its words contradict one another. And why did they not hide it? They said: We reflected as to the book of *Ecclesiastes,* and we found a reconciliation. So here, too, we may find a reconciliation. Let us search. It is written: (*Proverbs* xxvi, 5) *Answer a fool according to his folly;* and it is written: (*Proverbs* xxvi, 4) *Answer not a fool according to his folly.* There is no contradiction here. The first speaks of matters of Law and the other speaks of matters worldly.

Once a man came before Rabbi and said to him: "Your wife belongs to me and your children they are mine." "Would you like to drink a glass of wine?" The man drank and burst. This proved that the man lied.

Rabbi's prayers were effective so that his sons were not declared bastards. When the Rabbi prayed he used to say: May it be Thy will, O Lord, our God, that you protect me this day from the insolent and from insolence.

WORDS of learning, what does it mean? For instance: One day Rabbi Gamaliel lectured: Woman is destined, in the future, to conceive every day, for it was said: (*Jeremiah* xxxi, 8) *The woman conceived and beareth simultaneously.* One of his pupils laughed at him and said: (*Ecclesiastes* i, 9) *There is no new thing under the sun.* Come and I will show you something like it in this world. He went out and showed him a hen.

The Rabbis taught: A man should always be as patient as Hillel, and not be hot tempered as Shamai. There is a story that two men made a wager to the effect that whoever will succeed in making Hillel angry would receive four hundred *Zuz.* Whereupon one said: I will make him angry. It was just Sabbath Eve, and Hillel was washing his hair. The man went to Hillel's house and at the door shouted: Is Hillel in? Is Hillel in? Hillel dressed himself and confronted the man and said: My son, what wishest thou? The man answered: I wish to ask you a question. You may ask it, my son. Why are the heads of Babylonians round? You have asked a great question, my son, answered Hillel. Because the midwives of the Babylonians are not very experienced. The man waited an hour and came back and shouted: Is Hillel in? Is Hillel in? Hillel dressed again and went out to him: What wishest thou, my son? I wish to ask a question, he said. Ask, my son, ask. Why are the eyes of the Tadmorenes inflamed? Thou hast asked a great question. Because they live in sandy places. The man waited another hour, went back and again shouted: Is Hillel in? Is Hillel in? Hillel dressed again and went out to him. What wishest thou, my son? I have a question to ask. Ask, my son, ask. Why are the feet of the Africans broad? Thou hast asked a great question, my son, answered Hillel. Because they live in watery marshes. Then the man said, I have many questions to ask of you, but fear that you will become angry. Whereupon Hillel adjusted his robes and sat down near him and said: Ask all the questions thou hast to ask. Then the man said: Art thou the Hillel that is Prince of Israel? If it is thee, then there should be no more men like thee in Israel. Why? asked Hillel. Because I lost four hundred *Zuz* through thee. Said Hillel, Be careful of thy temper. Hillel is worth that because of him thou shouldst lose four hundred *Zuz* and many times four hundred. But thou canst not make Hillel lose his patience.

THE Rabbis taught: There is the story of a Heathen who came before Shamai and said: How many *Torahs* have you? Shamai answered: Two, the written law and the oral law. The Heathen said: I believe you as regards the written law but not as regards the oral law. Convert me, but on condition that you teach me the written law only. Shamai scolded him and sent him away with an insult. He went to Hillel, and Hillel received him with courtesy. The first day he taught him: Aleph, Beth, Gimmel, Daleth. The next day Hillel reversed the order. The Heathen said: Yesterday you did not teach me this way. Hillel replied: You see that you have to rely on me, so you must rely on me as regards the oral law, too.

There is another story of a heathen who approached Shamai and asked that he convert him and teach him the law for as long as he could stand on one foot; he repulsed him with a ruler that was in his hand.

The heathen went to Hillel. Hillel said to him: What is not right for thee, do not unto thy neighbor. This is the whole *Torah*. All the rest is only a commentary on this; go and learn it. Thus Hillel converted him.

Then there is the story of a heathen who passed near the Academy and heard one of the teachers recite: (*Exodus* xxviii, 4) *And these are the garments which they shall make; a breastplate, and an ephod.* Then he asked for whom are these garments. He was told that these are for the High Priest. Then he said: I'll go and become a Jew, so that I shall be made High Priest. He went to Shamai and said: Convert me to Judaism, so that I may be appointed High Priest. But he repulsed him with the ruler. He then went to Hillel. Hillel converted him, and said to him: Does a man become a King unless he knows the rules and conduct of government? Go and study the rules and laws of government. He went and read. When he came to: (*Numbers* i, 51) *And the stranger that cometh nigh shall be put to death,* he asked, to whom does this refer? Even to King David, he was answered. So the proselyte reasoned it out for himself. If this refers to the Jews who are called the children of the Lord, and because of his love towards them he called them: (*Exodus* iv, 22) *Israel is my son, even my first born,* and still it is written: *And the stranger that cometh nigh shall be put to death.* How much more an unworthy proselyte, who comes from nowhere with his walking stick and his bag. He came before Shamai and said: Am I fitted to become a High Priest? Isn't it written in the law: *And the stranger that cometh nigh shall be put to death?* He came before Hillel and said: Patient Hillel, may blessings come upon thee, that you brought me under the wings of the *Shekinah*.

Some time later, the three men met in one place and they said: Shamai's hot temper was ready to drive us out of this world, but Hillel's patience brought us under the wings of the *Shekinah*. (*Gemara*)

FOR three transgressions women die at childbirth: For laxity during the period of menstruation, for laxity in the Dough Offering, and for laxity in lighting of the Sabbath candles. (*Mishna*)

WHY just at childbirth? Raba answered: If the ox fell, then sharpen the knife. Abaya said: The bond-maid may increase her disobedience, she will be punished with the same rod. Rab Hisda said: Let the drunkard alone, he will fall of himself. Mar Ukba said: When the shepherd is lame, and the sheep run fast, there will be words at the gate, and in the barn there is the reckoning. At the gate of the shop there are brothers and friends aplenty, but at the toll gate there are neither brothers nor friends.

And when are men taken to task? Resh Lakish said: When they pass over a bridge. Only when they pass a bridge, no other time? Say, instances similar to a bridge. Rab would never cross a bridge when a pagan was on it. He said: Perhaps the judgment of the Lord will come upon him at this moment, and I shall be taken along. Samuel, on the other hand, would never cross a bridge unless a pagan was on it. He said: Satan has no power over two nations at one and the same time. Rabbi Yanai would examine the bridge first, and then he would cross it. Yanai expounded his opinion. He said: A man should never put himself in a dangerous position and say that a miracle will be performed for him, lest it be not performed. And if a miracle is performed, it will be deducted from his merited rewards.

The Rabbis taught: If one becomes ill and is near death, he is told to make his confession, for all who are sentenced to death are told to make their confession. If he goes out in the street, he should imagine that he is given into the custody of an officer. If he has a headache, he should imagine that he is put in irons. If he is confined to bed, he should feel as if he is put on a scaffold to be judged. For whoever is judged at the scaffold, if he has a great advocate he is saved, but if he has none, he is not saved. And these are a man's advocates: Repentence and good deeds. And if nine hundred and ninety-nine vote for his punishment, while one favors him, he is saved. For it was said: (*Job* xxxiii, 23) *If there be a messenger with him, an interpreter, one among a thousand, to show unto man his uprightness; Then he is gracious unto him, and saith, Deliver him from going down to the pit.*   (*Gemara*)

FROM CHAPTER II

WITH what may a woman go out on the Sabbath, and with what may she not go out? A woman shall not go out with braids of wool or braids of linen, or with straps on her head. And she must not take a bath with them, unless she has loosened them. And she must not go out with frontlets or hair ornaments unless they are sewed on. Nor shall she go into the street in a hairnet, nor with a gold tiara on her head, nor with necklaces, nor with earrings or a finger ring without a seal, nor with a needle that has no eye; but if she did go out with them, she need not bring the sin offering.

A man shall not go out with a nail-shod sandal, nor with one sandal if his foot is not injured, nor with phylacteries, nor with an amulet that has not been made by an expert, nor in armor, nor in a helmet, nor with greaves; but if he did go out with them, he need not bring a sin offering.

A woman shall not go out with a needle that has an eye, nor with a ring that bears a seal, nor with a brooch, nor a compact, nor with a bottle of perfume; and if she did go out with them, she must bring the sin offering. This is the opinion of Rabbi Meir, but the Sages say that in the case of a compact or a bottle of perfume she need not bring the sin offering.

A man shall not go out with a sword, nor with a bow, nor a shield, nor a lance, nor a spear; and if he did go out with them, he is guilty and must bring a sin offering. Rabbi Eleazer says: They are only his ornaments, but the Sages say these are a disgrace to him. For it was said: (*Isaiah* ii, 4) *And they shall beat their swords into plowshares, and their spears into pruning hooks. Nation shall not lift up sword against nation, neither shall they learn war any more.* A garter is clean, and one may go out with it on the Sabbath; ankle bracelets are unclean and one must not go out with them on the Sabbath.

A woman may go out with braids made of hair, whether they are her own or the hair of another, or made of animal hair, or with frontlets or head ornaments if they are sewed on; she may go out with a hair net or with false locks if she does not venture beyond the court yard. She may go out with the wool in her ears or the wool in her sandals, or with the wool that she prepared for her menstruation, or with a peppercorn or salt tablet, or anything that is taken in her mouth, but she must put it in her mouth before the Sabbath, and if it should fall out of her mouth, she must not put it back. Rabbi permits a false tooth or a gold tooth, but the Sages forbid it.

She may go out with a coin on her bunion. Young girls may go out with threads or even chips in their ears. Arabian women may go out veiled and Medean with their cloaks over their shoulder, and so may anyone. The Sages had in their mind the customs of the time.

A woman may knot her cloak over a stone or a nut or a coin so long as she does not knot it on the Sabbath.

Boys may go out with bindings, princes with bells, and so may anyone; the Sages referred, here, to the customs of the time.

One may go out with a locust's egg, or a fox's tooth, or a nail from the gallows as a charm. This is the opinion of Rabbi Meir, but the Sages forbid it even on weekdays because these are the ways of the pagan Amorites.   (*Mishna*)

FROM CHAPTER VI

THE main labors are forty less one: Sowing, ploughing, reaping, binding sheaves, threshing, winnowing, sorting, grinding, sifting, kneading, baking, shearing of wool, or bleaching, or shredding and dyeing, spinning, weaving, making two lintzen, weaving two threads, splitting two threads, knotting and unknotting, sewing two stitches, and ripping in order to sew, hunting a deer, slaughtering and skinning or salting, or curing its skin, scraping or cutting, writing two letters, erasing in order to write two letters, building or demolishing, extinguishing and lighting, hammering and carrying out things from one domain into another. These are the main labors, forty less one. (*Mishna*)

A TANNA taught: Sowing, pruning, planting, bending, and grafting, all are one kind of labor.

Ploughing, digging, trenching, they are all one class of work. Rabbi Shesheth said: If one has a mound and takes it down, if he removes it to his house, he is guilty of building; if in the field he is guilty of ploughing. If one fills in a ditch in the house, he is building; if in the field, he is ploughing.

We learned: Reaping, wire-making, sheaf-binding, are all one class of work.

Raba said: He who takes out salt of a salt pit is guilty of sheaf-binding. Abaya says: Sheaf-binding applies only to produce of the earth.

Threshing: We learned: Threshing, beating, scattering, they are all one class of work. (*Gemara*)

FROM CHAPTER VII

RABBI Yehuda said, in the name of Rab: Of all the things that the Holy One, blessed be He, created in His world, He did not create a thing for naught. He created the snail as a cure for a wound, the fly against the wasp, the mosquito against the snake, the snake against the eruption, the spider against the scorpion. How do you proceed with it? You take a black one and a white one and cook them together and you rub with it.

The Rabbis taught: There are five fears that the weak exert on the strong. The maphgia (an African gnat) over the lion, the gnat over the elephant, the fear of the scorpion for the spider, the eagle for the swallow, and the fear of the Leviathan for the Kilbith. Said Rab Yehuda in the name of Rab: What verse refers to this? (*Amos* v, 9) *That strengthen the despoiled over the strong.*

Rabbi Zera met Rab Yehuda at the door of his father-in-law and noticed that he was in a very cheerful mood, and if he would ask him all the secrets of the world he would be answered. So he asked him: Why do the goats go in front and the sheep in the rear? He told him: It is according to creation, first it was darkness and then there was light. Why is it that one species are covered and the other are not? Those which cover us are themselves covered, but those that cover not us are uncovered. Why is the tail of a camel short? Because it eats thorns. Why is the tail of an ox long? Because it grazes in the meadows and must beat off the gnats. Why is the proboscis of a locust soft? Because it lives among the willows, and if it were hard it would break off, and the locust would be blind.   (*Gemara*)

FROM CHAPTER VIII

Passover

(TRACTATE PESSAHIM)

ON THE eve of the fourteenth (of Nisan) a search for leavened matter is conducted by the light of a candle. Any place where leavened matter is not brought in does not require searching. Why was it said that in the cellar, two rows must be searched? Because it is a place where leavened matter might be brought in. The House of Shamai says: Two rows of the whole cellar must be searched. But the House of Hillel says only the two outer rows, the top rows. (*Mishna*)

RABBI Nahman ben Isaac said: We learned; every one is relied upon for the search for leavened matter, even women, slaves, and children. Why is that? For it is taken for granted that the house has been searched. It is the view of the learned that all are brothers as regards the searching for leavened matter. And we learned that if a brother dies and leaves a storehouse full of produce even if it be but one day old, it is presumed that the produce has been tithed. (*Gemara*)

FROM CHAPTER I

79

AS LONG as one is permitted to eat leaven, one may feed it to the cattle, to beasts and to birds, and one may sell it to a stranger, and may enjoy any benefit of it. But if the time of eating leaven has passed, he is barred from enjoying it. He may not heat an oven or a stove with it. Rab Yehuda says: "There is only one way of disposing of leaven—burning it." But the sages say: It can be shredded and scattered to the winds or thrown into the sea.   (*Mishna*)

AND he may sell it to a stranger. This is obvious. It contradicts the view of the Tanna who said: The House of Shamai taught: A man must not sell his leaven matter to a stranger unless he knows that it will be eaten before the Passover. But the House of Hillel says: As long as one may eat it, he may sell it.   (*Gemara*)

The leaven of a Gentile that has remained after Passover is permitted to a Jew. But one must not use the leaven of a Jew that has remained over Passover. Because it was said: (*Exodus* xiii, 7) *Neither shall be leaven seen with thee.*

These are the things with which a man discharges his duties with regard to leavened bread on Passover: Wheat, barley, spelt, rye and oats.

And these are the herbs with which a man discharges his duties on Passover: lettuce, chicory, mimosa, endive, and bitter herbs whether they are fresh or dried, but not if they are pickled or stewed or cooked. He fulfills his obligations who consumes the stalks only.

Bran for the chickens must not be soaked, but may be scalded.

One may not chew wheat and put it on his wound, because it will ferment. The Passover sacrifice may not be boiled in liquids or in fruit juices, but it may be basted with them, or dipped in them. Water that was used by a baker must be poured out, because it will ferment.

(Mishna)

ONLY with these, but not with rice and millet. Why these? Rabbi Simon ben Lakish answered: And thus taught the schools of Rabbi Ishmael and of Rabbi Eliezer ben Jacob. It was written: (*Deuteronomy* xvi, 3) *Thou shalt eat no leavened bread with it; seven days shalt thou eat unleavened bread therewith.* With foods that come to be leavened, one discharges his duty by eating unleavened bread made thereof, but those that do not become leavened, but decay, are excluded.

Thus the *Mishnah* does not agree with Rabbi Yohanan ben Nuri, who teaches that rice is a species of corn, and if one eats it in the leavened state, one is found guilty. For it was taught: Rabbi Yohanan ben Nuri forbids rice and millet because it is near leaven. A question was asked: Does near leaven mean that it becomes leavened quickly, or is it meant that it is near leaven, but never becomes leaven?

Rabbi Akiba is of the opinion that dough kneaded with milk, wine, oil or honey may not be used. Indeed, we were taught: Dough must not be kneaded on the Passover with wine, oil or honey; if it was kneaded, in accordance with Rabbi Gamaliel, it must be burned at once. But the sages say it may be eaten. Rabbi Akiba related: When I spent a week with Rabbi Eliezer and Rabbi Joshua, I kneaded for them dough with wine, oil and

honey, and they said nothing. Though one must not
knead, one may smooth the surface with them. This is
in accordance with the first *Tanna*. The sages say: With
that milk which one may knead, one may smooth; and
they all agree that one must not knead with warm water.
There is no controversy here; one speaks of the first day
of the Festival while the other speaks of the second day.
Thus said Rabbi Joshua to his sons: On the first, knead
not for me with milk, but from then on you may knead
for me with milk. But it was taught: One must not knead
dough with milk, and if one kneaded with milk, the whole
loaf is forbidden. This is a precaution because one may
get the habit of transgression. Rather, he said thus:
Knead not for me with honey on the first day, and knead
not for me with honey from then on. If you wish you
may say that he spoke thus of milk.   (*Gemara*)

FROM CHAPTER II

THESE are the things that must be removed on Passover: Babylonian curds, Medean beer, Edomite vinegar,
Egyptian beer, dyer's brew, cook's starch, and the paste
of scribes. Rabbi Eliezer says: Women's ornaments also.
And this is the rule: Everything that was made of any
grain must be removed for Passover. These are forbidden as a precaution but they do not incur death penalty.
(*Mishna*)

THREE things were said about Babylonian curds:
It stupefies the mind, blinds the eye and weakens the
body. It stupefies the mind through the acid; it blinds
the eye through the salt, and it weakens the body through
the mould.

The Rabbis taught: Three things accelerate the bowels, bend the stature, and take away five-hundredths of the eyesight. These are: Coarse bread, raw alcohol and raw cabbage. The Rabbis taught: Three things decrease the movement of the bowels and straighten the stature, and light up the eyes, and these are: Light bread, fatty meat, and old wine. Light bread from fine flour; fatty meat from a goat that was mated; old wine, very old. Everything that may be good for one organ may be harmful for another, and what is harmful for one organ may be good for another. But ginger, long peppers, light bread and fat meat are good for the whole body. "Medean beer" because barley is mixed into it. "Edomite vinegar" because grain is mixed with it. Rabbi Nahman ben Isaac said: At first, when wine for libation was brought from Judea, it never turned to vinegar, unless grain was mixed into it, and that was known as plain vinegar. But now the wine of the Edomites does not turn into vinegar unless grain is mixed into it, and it is called "Edomite vinegar." This is to fulfill the scripture: (*Ezekiel* xxvi, 2) *I shall be replenished, now she is laid waste.* If one is full, the one is waste. If the other is waste, this one is full. Rabbi Nahman ben Isaac used to say: (*Gen.* xxv, 23) *And the one people shall be stronger than the other people.* (*Gemara*)

IF THE fourteenth falls on the Sabbath, the leaven is removed before the Sabbath. Those are the words of Rabbi Meir. But the sages say: They are removed in their usual time. Rabbi Eliezer bar Zadok said: Heave-offering is removed before Sabbath, but ordinary food in its usual time. (*Mishna*)

IT WAS taught: Rabbi Eliezer bar Zadok said: Father
once spent a Sabbath, on which the fourteenth fell, in
Yabneh. When Zonin, one of Rabbi Gamaliel's officers,
came in and announced: The time has come to remove
the leaven, I went along with father and we removed
the leaven.   (*Gemara*)

IF ONE is on his way to slaughter his Paschal-Offer-
ing, or to circumcise his son, or to partake of the betrothal feast at his father-in-law's house, and he remembered that he left the unleavened in his home, if he has
time to go back and remove it, and then return to fulfill the precept, he should go back and remove the leaven;
but if he has not time enough to fulfill both, he should
annul the leaven in his heart. If he is on the way to res-
cue someone from an enemy troop, from a flood, from
robbers, from a fire, or from a collapsing structure, he
should annul it in his heart. But if he went out just for
the enjoyment of the Sabbath he must return at once.
                                              (*Mishna*)

I WILL point out a contradiction. If he is on the way
to partake of the betrothal feast in his father-in-law's
house, or for the enjoyment of the Sabbath, he must go
back at once. Rabbi Yohanan said: There is no contradiction here: One speaks of the view of Rabbi Yehuda,
the other of the view of Rabbi Yosi. For we were taught:
The betrothal meal is a voluntary function. These are
the words of Rabbi Yehuda; but Rabbi Yosi says: It
is a precept. However, Rab Hisda says: The argument
here refers only to the second feast, because as to the
first feast, all agree that it is a religious precept. You

may, even, say that both views are those of Rabbi Yehuda, for there is no contradiction here; one refers to
the first feast while the other refers to the second. It
was taught: Rabbi Yehuda said: I heard only of the betrothal feast, but not as regards the feast of the gifts.
Rabbi Yosi said: I heard as regards the betrothal feast
and the feast of the gifts.

It was taught: Rabbi Simon said: A scholar must
not enjoy himself at a feast which is not of a religious
character. What is a feast of this kind? Said Rabbi
Yohanan, for instance: The betrothal of a daughter of
an Israelite to the daughter of a Priest, or the daughter of a scholar to that of an ignoramus. For Rabbi
Yohanan said: The marriage of the daughter of a priest
and the daughter of an Israelite will not bring good re-
sults. How so? Rab Hisda answered: She will either
become a widow, or a divorcee, or she will have no children. We learned in a *Baraitha*: Either he will bury
her or she will bury him, or she will bring poverty upon
him. But this is not so. For Rabbi Yohanan said: If
one wants to become rich, he should join the seed of
Aaron, for the *Torah* and the priesthood will enrich
them. There is no controversy here. One refers to a
scholar and the other to an ignoramus.

Rabbi Joshua was married to a priest's daughter.
When he fell sick once, he said: Aaron is not pleased that
I joined his seed and that he should have a son-in-law
like me. Rabbi Idis ben Abin was married to a daughter
of a priest, and he had two ordained sons: Rabbi Shesheth ben Rabbi Idis and Rabbi Joshua ben Idis. Rab Papa
said: Had I not married a priest's daughter, I would
not have become rich. Rabbi Kahana said: Had I not

married the daughter of a priest, I would not be exiled, but he was answered: You were exiled to a place of learning. He answered: But I was not exiled the way other people were exiled.

Rabbi Isaac said: Whoever partakes of general feasts, will eventually be exiled, for it was said: (*Amos* vi, 4) *And eat the lambs out of the flock, and the calves out of the midst of the stall.* And it was said: (*Amos* vi, 7) *Therefore now shall they go captive with the first that go captive.*

The Rabbis taught: A scholar that makes it a habit of eating in every place, will at the end destroy his home, bring widowhood upon his wife, and make his children orphans. He will forget his learning, will be given up to many quarrels. His words will be unheard. He will desecrate the Name of Heaven, the name of his teacher, and the name of his father, and will attach a bad name to himself, to his children and to his children's children, to the end of all generations. In what way? Abaya said: He will be called the son of the glutton. Rabbi said: He will be called a son of a "Tavern Dancer." Rab Papa said: He will be called the son of a "Plate Licker." Rabbi Shemaiah said: The son of a man who sleeps in his clothes.

The Rabbis taught: A man should sell all he possesses and marry the daughter of a scholar, for if he dies or goes into exile, he may be sure that his children will become scholars. But he should not marry the daughter of an ignoramus, for if he dies or goes into exile, his children will be ignorant.

The Rabbis taught: A man should sell all he possesses and marry the daughter of a scholar, or marry

off his daughter to a scholar. This compares to the
grafting of grapes with grapes—a good and acceptable
thing. But he should not marry a daughter of an ignoramus. This compares to the grafting of grapes with
thorny berries, which is a detestable and an unacceptable
thing.

The Rabbis taught: A man should sell all he possesses, and he should marry a daughter of a scholar. If
he can not find the daughter of a scholar, he should marry
a daughter of a distinguished man of his generation;
if he can not find the daughter of a distinguished man,
he should marry the daughter of the head of a synagogue; if he can not find a daughter of the head of a
synagogue, he should marry the daughter of a head of
a charitable organization; if he can not find a daughter
of a head of a charitable organization, he should marry
the daughter of an elementary school teacher, but he
should never marry the daughter of an ignoramus. For
they are detestable, their wives are vermin, and of their
daughters it was said: (*Deuteronomy* xxvii, 21) *Cursed
be he that lieth with any manner of beast.*

Rabbi Akiba said: When I was an ignoramus, I used
to say: Who would give a scholar into my hands, I would
bite him like an ass. His disciples said to him: Rabbi,
say like a dog. He answered: The first bites and breaks
the bone, while the other bites, but does not break the
bone.

Rabbi Meir used to say: If one marries off his daughter to an ignoramus, it is as if he bound her and laid her
before a lion. A lion falls on his prey and devours it,
and has no shame. So an ignoramus beats her and mates
with her and has no shame.

Rabbi Eliezer said: If they did not need us for trad-
ing with us, they would kill us. Rabbi Hiya taught:
If one studies the Torah before an ignoramus, it is as if
he mated with his wife in front of him. For it was said:
(*Deuteronomy* xxxiii, 4) *Moses commanded us a law
the inheritance* (MORASHAH) *of the congregation of
Jacob.* Read not MORASHAH but ME'ORASHAH (betrothed). The hatred of the ignorant towards the
learned is greater than the hatred of the Gentiles toward
the Jews, and their wives are even worse.

We learned: He that studied and foresook his studies,
hates the scholar with more hate than anyone else.

Six things were said of the ignorant: One does not
commit testimony to them, and one does not take their
testimony; one does not reveal a secret to them; one does
not appoint them as guardians for orphans; one does
not appoint them as guardians of charity chests, and
one does not join their company on a trip.   (*Gemara*)

FROM CHAPTER III

WHERE the custom is to work on Passover eve until
midday one may work until midday, but in a place where
the custom is not to work, one must not work.

If a man went from a place where the custom is not
to work to a place where the custom is to work, or from
a place where the custom is to work to a place where
the custom is not to work, he is bound by the stricter
custom of the place whence he came, or to the stricter
custom of the place to which he has come. But on no
account must he act differently from the local custom,
because it may lead to strife.   (*Mishna*)

WHY only on Passover eve? This should refer even to Sabbath eve, or the eve of other festivals. For we learned: Whoever does work on Sabbath eve or on the eves of Festivals, from afternoon prayers onward, shall never see a sign of blessing. There it is said: Only "after" the afternoon prayer he is forbidden to do work, but not "near" the afternoon prayer. But here it is said: From midday on. Then, there he merely sees no sign of blessing, but he is not banned, but here he is placed under the ban.

The Rabbis taught: Some are industrious and profit by it, but others are industrious and incur a loss. One is lowly and profits by it, another is lowly and incurs a loss. One is industrious and profits when he works the whole week but not on Sabbath eve. But another is industrious and incurs a loss, when he works the whole week and on Sabbath eve. A lowly man who profits is he who does not work the whole week and does not work on Sabbath eve. A lowly man who incurs a loss is one who does not work the whole week but works on Sabbath eve.

The Rabbis taught: Whosoever looks for his wife's earning and working at the mill, shall never see a sign of blessing. "The earnings of his wife" means through peddling. "At the mill" means through hiring her out. But a woman who makes things and sells them is praised in the *Scripture,* for it was written: (*Proverbs* xxxi, 24) *She maketh fine linen and selleth it.*

The Rabbis taught: Street peddlers and breeders of small cattle, and those who cut down good trees, and those who grab the best portion, will never see a sign

of blessing. Why? For people will always gaze at
them.

In four instances there is no sign of blessing to be
found: The earnings of scribes, the earnings of interpreters, and the earnings of orphans, and moneys that
come from overseas. Why the interpreter? The reason
is that it is like earnings for Sabbath work. So are also
the wages of orphans, for these cannot be legally re-
nounced. So are the moneys that come from overseas,
because a miracle cannot be performed every day. But
why of the scribes? Rabbi Joshua ben Levi answered:
The sages of the great assembly spent twenty-four days
in fasting and prayer, so that the scribes should not grow
rich. For if they become rich they will stop writing.

Those who write books, phylacteries and *Mezuzoth,*
their traders, and their traders' traders, and all who deal
in sacred articles, and this includes traders in blue wool
for praying shawls, never see a sign of blessing, but if
they engage in them for the sake of the Lord, they will
see a sign of blessing.   (*Gemara*)

IN A place where the practice was to eat roast meat
on Passover night, one should eat roast meat; where the
custom is not to eat, one must not eat it.

In a place where the custom is to light the candles on
the eve of the Day of Atonement, one may light them;
wherever the custom is not to light them, one does not
light them. But one lights the candles in the synagogue,
in the house of study, in dark alleys and near a sick person.

Where it is the custom to work on the ninth of Ab,

one may work. In a place where the custom is not to work, one must not work. And in all places scholars must not work. Rabbi Gamaliel says: A man should always make a scholar of himself. The sages said: In Judea, they worked on Passover eve till noon; but in Galilee, they did not work at all. As to work on the night of the fourteenth, the House of Shamai forbid it, but the House of Hillel permit it until dawn.

The men of Jericho inaugurated six things; for three they were not reproved; for three they were reproved; and these are the things for which they were not reproved: They grafted date palms all day long; they pattered the "Hear O Irael," and they reaped and stacked the produce before the Omer Offering. And for the following they were reproved: They were permitted the fruit of sanctified trees, they ate fallen fruit from under the trees on the Sabbath, and they gave tithes from green vegetables. For these the sages reproved them.   (*Mishna*)

KING Hezekiah did six things. With three, the sages agreed; and with three, they disagreed. He dragged the bones of his father on a bier made of ropes, and the sages approved of it. He demolished the copper serpent, and they approved of it. He hid away the book of cures and they approved of it. And of three things they did not approve. He took down the doors of the Temple and sent them to the King of Assyria, and they did not approve of it. He dammed the waters of the Upper Gihon, and they did not approve of it. He lengthened the month of Nisan, and they did not approve of it.   (*Baraitah*)

FROM CHAPTER IV

THE Passover offering is slaughtered in three divisions. For it was said: (*Exodus* xii, 6) *And the whole assembly of the congregation of Israel shall kill it.* "Assembly", "Congregation", and "Israel". The first division entered; the Temple court was filled. Whereupon the gates of the court were closed. Then they sounded the horn, first sustained, then stacatto, and then sustained. The priests stood in rows, and in their hands they held silver basins and basins of gold. A row that was of silver was entirely of silver, and a row that was of gold was entirely of gold. They did not mix them. The basins had round bottoms, so that they could not be set down, so that the blood would not congeal. An Israelite slaughtered his offering, the priest took the blood and passed it to the next one, and this one to the next. He received the full one and returned the empty. The priest that was nearest the altar tossed it in one throw at the base of the altar.

When the first division came out, the second division entered, when the second came out, the third entered. As the procedure was with the first group, so it was with the second, and so with the third. They recited "Hallelujah". If they finished it they repeated it and if they finished it a second time, they recited it a third time, although they never completed it a third time. The third division never reached as far as: (*Psalms* cxvi, 1) *I love the Lord because he hath heard.* For the people were not many. As the procedure took place on week days, so it was also on the Sabbath. Except that the priest swilled the Temple court; this against the wishes of the Sages. Rabbi Yehuda said: They would fill a cup of the

mixed blood and make one toss at the altar. But the
Sages did not approve of it.

When the carcass was opened, the Israelite removed
the portion to be sacrificed. He put it on a tray and
handed it to the priest to be burned at the altar. The
first division went out and sat on the Temple mount.
The second sat on the rampart, and the third remained
where they were. When it got dark, they went out and
roasted their Paschal Offering.   (*Mishna*)

SAID Rabbi Isaac: The Paschal offering is not slaughtered unless there are three groups of thirty men.
What is the reason? "Assembly", "Congregation" and
"Israel" are mentioned. We are not sure whether it
means all together or one after the other. Therefore,
we need three groups of thirty each, so that we will have
at the same time three groups, and three following each
other. In that case, fifty are also sufficient. First thirty
enter and perform the ritual, then ten enter, and ten
follow them.

No one was ever crushed in the Temple court on
Passover, except once in the time of Hillel. An old man
was crushed, and this was known as the Passover of the
Crushed.

King Agrippa once wanted to count the hosts of
Israel. So he said to the High Priest: Count the Paschal
Offerings. Whereupon the priest took a kidney from
each lamb. And there were six hundred thousand pairs
of kidneys, double the number of those that went out of
Egypt. And that excluded those who were away on a
journey and those who were unclean. And at least ten

people were registered for each sacrificed lamb. This was called the Passover of the Throngs. (*Gemara*)

HOW is the Paschal lamb roasted? One brings a skewer of pomegranate wood, and inserts it through the mouth to the buttocks and puts the knees and the entrails inside of it. These are the words of Rabbi Yosi, the Galilean. Rabbi Akiba said: This is not roasting, it's boiling; the knees and the entrails are hung outside of it.

The Paschal offering must not be roasted on a metal spit, nor on a grill. Rabbi Zadok said: It happened once that Rabbi Gamaliel said to his slave Tabi: Go out and roast the Paschal lamb on a grill, but if it touched the earthen ware of the oven, he had to cut off that part.

(*Mishna*)

THE word of the Lord that came unto Hosea, the son of Beeri, in the days of Uzziah, Jotham, Ahaz and Hezekiah, Kings of Judea. (Hosea i, 1.)

Four prophets prophesied in one period and Hosea was the eldest of all of them. For it was said: (*Hosea* i, 2) *The Lord spake first to Hosea.* Indeed, did he speak to Hosea first? Were there not many other prophets from Moses to Hosea? Said Rabbi Yohanan: First of the four prophets that were prophesying in that period. These were: Hosea, Isaiah, Amos and Micah. Said the Holy One, blessed be He, to Hosea: Thy children have sinned. He should have replied: These are Thy children, the seed of Abraham, Isaac and Jacob. Favor them with Thy mercy. Not only did he not say this, but he said to the Lord: Lord of the universe, the whole world is Thine. Exchange them for another Nation. The Lord, blessed be He, said to him: What shall I do to this old man? Shall I tell him: Go and take a harlot and she will bear thee children of harlotry, and then I shall tell him: Send them away from thy presence. If he will be able to send them away, then I, too, shall send Israel away; as it was said: (*Hosea* i, 2) *And the Lord said to Hosea, go take unto thee a wife of whoredom and children of whoredom.* And it was written (*Ibid.* 3): *So he went and took Gomer, the daughter of Diblain.* Gomer explained Rab: All completed their lust with her; *Gomer* means finished. The daughter of *Diblain* means the daughter of ill repute from the word *diba,* (talk). Samuel said: She was sweet to everyone like a fig. (*Debelah.*) Rabbi Yohanan said: That all pressed upon her like a pressed fig. Another interpretation of *Gomer* is that of Rabbi Yehuda. He said: In those days they wanted to make a finish (*Gomer*) of the wealth of Israel. Rabbi Yohanan said: Indeed, they robbed and made a finish. For it was said: (2 *Kings* xiii, 7) *Syria had destroyed them, and had made them like the dust by threshing.*

Conceived and bare him a son, and the Lord said unto him, Call his name Jezreel; for yet a little while, and I will avenge the blood of Jezreel upon the house of Je-hu, and will cause to cease the Kingdom of the house of Israel. And it shall come to pass at that day, that I will break the bow of Israel in the valley of Jezreel. And she conceived again, and bare a daughter. And God said unto him, call her name Lo-ruhama (no mercy) for I will no more have mercy upon the house of Israel; but I will utterly take them away.

*She conceived and bare a son. Then said God, call
his name Lo-ami (not my people): for ye are not my
people, and I will not be your God. (Hosea* i, 3-9.)

After two sons and a daughter were born to him,
the Lord, blessed be He, said to Hosea: Thou shouldst
learn from Thy teacher, Moses. For when I spoke to
him, he separated from his wife. Thou, too, shouldst
separate from thine wife. Said he: Lord of the Universe, I have children by her, and I cannot send her
away nor divorce her. Said the Holy One, blessed be
He: Now thou, whose wife is a harlot and thy children
are children of harlotry, and thou knowest not whether
they are thine children or children of other men: thou art
so. Now Israel, who are my children whom I have tried,
the seed of Abraham, Isaac and Jacob, one of the three
possessions that I treasure in this world—One possession is the *Torah.* For it is written: (*Proverbs* viii, 22)
The Lord possessed me in the beginning of his way.
Heaven and earth is one possession, as it was written:
(*Gen.* xiv, 19) *Possessor of heaven and earth.* Israel
is one possession, for it is written: (*Exodus* xv, 16)
*People—which thou has purchased—*And thou sayest:
Exchange them for another nation. When Hosea saw
that he had transgressed, he arose and begged for mercy
for himself. Said the Lord to him: Instead of begging
for mercy for thyself, thou shouldst ask mercy for Israel,
against whom I decreed three decrees because of thee.
Hosea arose and pleaded for mercy for Israel, and the
Lord voided the decrees. Then He blessed them.

RABA said: The world is six thousand parsangs, and
the density of the skies is one thousand parsangs. The

first is a tradition: the second is logic. This is in accord with Rabbi ben Bar Hanah, who said in the name
of Rabbi Yohanan: An average man travels ten parsangs
in one day; from dawn to the rising of the sun five
miles; from sunset to the appearance of stars also five
miles. Thus we find that the thickness of the skies is
one sixth of a day's journey.

Come and hear: Egypt is four hundred square parsangs. Now Egypt is one sixtieth of Ethiopia, and
Ethiopia is one sixtieth of the world, and the world is one
sixtieth of the Garden, and the Garden is one sixtieth
of Eden, and Eden one sixtieth of Hell. Thus we find
that the whole world is like the lid of a pot to Hell.
Though this is not so.

Come and hear: Rabbi Nathan said: The whole continent is situated under one star. We know that a man
looks at a star while he is walking east. He finds himself opposite the star, and when he walks in the direc-
tion of the four corners of the world, it is also opposite
him. Therefore, the whole continent must be under one
star. This, too, can be disproved.

The Rabbis taught: The circle is fixed, while the
constellations revolve. While the Sages of the world
maintain that the circle revolves while the constellations
are fixed. Rabbi said: Their view is wrong. We never
find the Waggon in the south and Scorpio in the north.
Rabbi Aha ben Jacob remarked: Perhaps this is like the
axis of a millstone, or a socket of a door.

The Sages of Israel say: The sun travels beneath the
sky during the day, and above the sky during the night,
while the Sages of the world maintain that the sun travels beneath the sky by day, and beneath the earth by

night. It seems that their opinion is better than ours
because during the day the wells are cool, but at night
they are warm.

Rabbi Nathan said: During the summer the sun
travels at the top of the sky; therefore the whole world
is hot, but the wells are cool, but during the rainy season the sun travels at the lower ends of the sky; the
whole world is cool, but the wells are warm.

The Rabbis taught: The sun travels over four
courses. During Nisan, Eyar and Sivan, it travels over
the mountains, so that it can melt the snows. During
Tamuz, Ab and Elul it travels over the earth, so that
it can ripen the fruits. During Thishri, Marheshvan,
and Kislev, it travels over the waters, so that it can dry
up the rivers. During Tabath, Shebath and Adar, it
travels over the desert, so that it won't dry up the seeds.

(*Gemara*)

FROM CHAPTER VIII

ON THE eve of Passover, from close to the afternoon offering, one must not eat a thing until nightfall.
Even the poorest in Israel then must not eat without re-
clining. And he must be allotted not less than four
glasses of wine, even if these have to come from the
charity kitchens.

The first cup of wine is served and according to the
House of Shamai one pronounces first the benediction
over the day, and then the benediction over the wine, but
the House of Hillel says first one pronounces the benediction over the wine, and then the benediction over the
day.

Then lettuce is set before one, and one eats the lettuce

dipped in vinegar or salt water, until he comes to the breaking of bread. The matzoh, lettuce and *haroseth* (a mixture of nuts, fruit, and wine) and two dishes are brought before him, though *haroseth* is not a religious precept. Rabbi Eliezer ben Zadok says: It is a religious precept; and in the days of the Temple they used to set before him the Paschal lamb.

Then the second glass of wine is poured out, and the son asks of his father; if the son has no understanding the father instructs him what to ask: Why is this night different from other nights? Every other night we eat either leavened or unleavened bread; tonight we eat only unleavened bread. Every other night we eat all kinds of green vegetables; tonight, only bitter greens. Every other night we eat meat either cooked, roasted or stewed; tonight, only roasted. Every other night we dip once; tonight we dip twice. And according to the understanding of the son, the father answers him. He begins with the disgrace and ends with the praise. He expounds: (*Deuteronomy* xxvi, 5) *A Syrian ready to perish was my father,* till he finishes the whole section.

Rabbi Gamaliel used to say: Whoever does not pronounce three things on Passover, does not discharge his obligations, and these are: Passover, Matzoh, and Bitter herbs. Passover—because the Lord passed over the houses of our fathers in Egypt. Matzoh—because our fathers were redeemed from Egypt. Bitter herbs—because the life of our fathers was made bitter in Egypt.

The third cup is poured out and one pronounces the benediction after the meal. Over the fourth cup one recites "Hallelujah", and then the benedictions over song. Between the cups if one wishes to drink, one may drink;

but one does not drink between the third and the fourth cup.

One must not feast again after partaking of the Paschal lamb.

If some fell asleep and awoke, they may eat, but if all fell asleep they may not eat again. Rabbi Yosi says: If they dozed off they may eat; but if they fell asleep, they must not eat again.   (*Mishna*)

WHY just mention on the eve of Passover? The same applies to the eves of Sabbath and Festivals. We were taught: On the eves of Sabbath and Festivals one must not eat after the Afternoon Offering, so that he may enter the Sabbath with an appetite. These are the words of Rabbi Yehuda. Rabbi Yosi says :He may keep on eating until nightfall. Rab Huna said: This exposition was necessitated because of Rabbi Yosi who taught: He may keep on eating until nightfall. This applies only to the eves of Sabbath and other Festivals, but as to the eve of Passover, it is distinctly understood that one must refrain, because of the obligation of eating unleavened bread. Rab Papa taught according to the view of Rab Yehuda: On the eves of Sabbath and Festivals one may not eat after the Afternoon Offering, while on the eve of Passover one is forbidden to eat close to the Afternoon Offering. Now, may one eat on the eves of Sabbath and Festivals close to the Afternoon Offering? Indeed we learned: A man must not eat on the eves of Sabbath and Festivals from the ninth hour on, so that he may enter the Sabbath with an appetite.

The Rabbis taught: Everyone is obligated to drink the four cups of wine—men, women, and children. What satisfaction do children get from wine, asked Rabbi Yehuda? They are given the roasted ears of corn and nuts so that they won't fall asleep, and will ask the questions. Rabbi Akiba used to give children roasted ears of corn and nuts on the eve of Passover, so that they would not fall asleep and would ask the questions.

Rabbi Eliezer said: One eats the Matzoh hurriedly on the night of Passover so that the children will not fall asleep. It was told of Rabbi Akiba, that he never said in the house of study: It is time to stop, except on the eves of Passover and the Day of Atonement. On the eve of Passover because of the children, so they would not fall asleep; and on the eve of the Day of Atonement so that the children may be fed.

The Rabbis taught: It is a man's duty to make his children and his household happy on the Festival, for it was said: (*Deuteronomy* xvi, 14) *And thou shalt rejoice in thy feast, thou, and thy son, and thy daughter, and thy manservant, and thy maidservant, and the Levite, the stranger, the fatherless, and the widow that are with in thy gates.*

With what does he make them happy? With wine. Rabbi Yehuda said: Men with what is right for men and women with what is proper for women. Men with what is proper for them—wine. And women with what? Rabbi Joseph said: In Babylonia they used to give brightly colored garments. In Palestine—linen garments beautifully starched and ironed.

Rabbi Yehuda ben Bathyra said: When the Temple was in existence, there was no rejoicing, but with meat, for it was said: (*Deuteronomy* xxvii, 7) *And thou shalt offer peace offerings, and shall eat there, and rejoice*

before the Lord thy God. But now that the Temple is
no more, there is no rejoicing except with wine. For it
was said: (*Psalms* civ, 15) *And wine that maketh glad
the heart of man.*

HE WHO suspends his bread basket in his house,
brings about poverty. For people say: He who suspends his bread basket, brings his food in suspense. However, this refers only to bread. Meat and fish are not
harmed. For that is the way to keep them. Bran in
the house leads to poverty. Crumbs in the house cause
poverty. On Sabbath nights and on Wednesdays the
demons rest upon them.

The genius of plenty is called "Cleanliness". The
genius of poverty is "Filth". Dirt in the spout of the
pitcher causes poverty. If one drinks from a saucer,
he is liable to a sty. If one eats cress without washing
his hands, he will experience fear for thirty days. If
one lets blood without washing his hands, he will experience fear for seven days. If one cuts his hair without
washing his hands, he will experience fear for three days.
If he cuts his nails without washing his hands he will be
afraid one day, without knowing why he is afraid.

Evil spirits rest on food and drink that is put under
the bed, even if it be covered with iron lids.

A man must not drink water from rivers and cisterns
at night. If he drinks, his blood is upon his own head,
because of the danger. What kind of danger? The
danger of the Shabriri, the demons of blindness. What
shall he do if he is thirsty? If there is someone with
him he says: So-and-so, the son of the So-and-so, I am
thirsty. But if there is no one, he says to himself: So-

and-so, my mother told me "Beware of the Shabriri".
Shabriri Briri, riri, yiri, ri. I want water in the white
cup.

"EVEN from the charity kitchen." Obviously. This
is necessary because of Rabbi Akiba who said: Make
your Sabbath like a weekday, but depend not on another
man. But in this instance he agrees because of the pub-
licity of the miracle.

Rabbi Akiba bequeaths seven things to his son Rabbi
Yehoshua. Do not dwell at the highest point of the
town, because of your studies. Do not dwell in a town
whose heads are scholars. Do not enter thine house
suddenly, and surely not the house of thy neighbor. Do
not leave shoes off thy feet. Arise early and eat; in the
summer before it gets hot, and in the winter before it gets
chilly. And make thy Sabbath like a weekday, but do not
ask aid of other people. And be on good terms with a
man on whom fortune smiles. Rabbi Papa said: This
does not mean that one buys from him or sells to him,
but that he enters into partnership with him.

SAID Rab to Rabbi Assi: Dwell not in a town where
no horses neigh, and no dogs bark. And dwell not in a
town whose head is a physician. And marry not two
women; but if you have married two, marry a third.

Said Rab to Rabbi Kahana: Turn an ass around in
the market place but turn not your words around. Skin
an ass in the market place, and earn your living; do not
say: I am a priest, I am a distinguished personage, and
this is beneath my dignity. If you ascend to the roof,
take provisions with you.

Melons may be a hundred for a *Zuz* in the town, but have them under your cloak.

Said Rab to his son, Hiya: Drink not medicines. Leap not over streams. Do not have teeth extracted, and provoke not a serpent nor a Syrian woman.

The Rabbis said: These three must not be provoked: A little heathen, a little snake, and a little pupil. Because they have their kingdom behind their ear.

Three things, said Rabbi Yehoshua ben Levi in the name of the men from Jerusalem: Frequent not the roofs, because of immoral scenes. If your daughter has attained puberty; free your slave and give her to him. And take heed of your wife and her first son-in-law. What is the reason? Rabbi Hisdu said: because of incest. Rabbi Kahana said: because of money. They are both right.

Of three, the Lord, blessed be He, proclaims every day: Of a bachelor who lives in a large city and does not sin; of a poor man who returns lost property to its owner; of a rich man who pays his tax without grumbling.

There are three who are beloved by the Holy One, blessed be He. He who never gets angry; he who never gets drunk, and he who does not insist on all his rights.

Three are hated by the Holy One, blessed be He: He who says one thing with his mouth, and another thing in his heart; he who possesses evidence in favor of his neighbor and does not testify for him; and he who saw an indecent act of his neighbor and is the only one to testify against him.

The Rabbis taught: The life of these three is no life: the compassionate, the hot-tempered and the fastidious. Said Rabbi Joseph: all these qualities are to be found in me.

Three hate one another: Dogs, chickens and partners. Some say: also prostitutes, and some say: The Babylonian scholars, too, hate one another.

Three love each other: The proselytes, the slaves, and the ravens. Four are impossible to put up with: A proud beggar, a rich man who lies, an old man who whores, and an Elder who lords it over the community. Some say: also one who divorces his wife and then remarries her.   (*Gemara*)

"ONE does not feast again after partaking of the Paschal Offering" (*Apikoman*).   (*Mishna*)

WHAT is meant by *Apikoman?* Rab says: One must not go from one Passover feast to another. Samuel says: It means, for example, eating mushrooms for me and young pigeons for Abba. Rabbi Hanina ben Shila and Rabbi Yohanan say: For example: Eating dates, roasted ears of corn, and nuts. It was taught according to Rabbi Yohanan: After the Paschal meal, one must not partake of dates, roasted ears of corn, or nuts.   (*Gemara*)

FROM CHAPTER X

The Day of Atonement

(TRACTATE YOMA)

S EVEN days before the Day of Atonement the High Priest was moved from his home into the Chamber of the officials.   And a substitute was prepared, lest something happen to him and disqualify him.   Rabbi Yehuda said: Another wife was also prepared for him, lest his wife die.   For it was said: (*Lev.* xvi, 6) *And make atonement for himself, and for his house.* "His house" —this is his wife.   Said they to him: If so, there is no end to the thing.

They appointed for him Elders from the Elders of the Court, who read before him of the order of the day, and they said to him: My Master, High Priest, read with thine own mouth, you might have forgotten, or you might have never learned.   On the eve of the Day of Atonement, early in the morning they put him at the Eastern Gate, and they passed before him oxen, rams, and sheep, so that he might get acquainted with and used to the service.

For the whole seven days they did not withhold from him any food or drink. But on the eve of the Day of Atonement, toward nightfall, they did not let him eat much, because too much food brings on sleep.

The Elder of the Court delivered him to the Elders of the priesthood and took him up to the House of Abtinas, and adjured and took leave from him and left. They said to him: My Master, High Priest, we are the delegates of the Court and thou art our delegate, and the delegate of the Court. We adjure you by Him who made His name dwell in this House, that thou change not aught of what we have told thee. He turns aside and weeps and they turn aside and weep. If he was a scholar he would preach, but if not, disciples of the Sages preached for him. If he was used to reading he would read, if not, they read for him. And what do they read for him? From *Job,* from *Ezra* and from *Chronicles.* Zecharaiah ben Kabutal said: Many times I have read for him from *Daniel.*   (*Mishna*)

"HE TURNS aside and weeps and they turn aside and weep." He turned aside and wept because he was suspected of being a Saduccee, and they turned aside and wept, for as Rabbi Joshua ben Levi said,—When someone suspects another who is guiltless, he will be punished bodily. What was all this about?—so that he would not arrange the incense outside and then bring it into the Holy of Holies, as the Saduccees were apt to do.

The Rabbis taught: There was once a Saduccee who arranged the incense outside and then brought it in. As he was departing he was very joyous. His father met him and said: Though we are Saduccees, we are afraid

of the Pharisees. Answered the son: My whole life I
was aggrieved over this verse. (*Lev.* xvi, 2) *For I will
appear in the cloud upon the mercy seat.* I thought,
when shall I have the opportunity to fulfill this? Now
that the opportunity has presented itself to me; should
I not have fulfilled it? It was related, that only a few
days later he was found dead, lying on a heap of refuse,
and worms were coming out of his nose. Some say he
was smitten as he was coming out. Rabbi Hiya said:
A noise was heard in the Temple Court. An angel came
and smote him in the face. When his brethren, the
priests, came upon him, they found imprints of a calf's
foot between his shoulders. For it was said: (*Ezekiel*
i, 7) *And their feet were straight feet; and the sole of
their feet was like the sole of a calf's foot.*

The Rabbis taught: Three sounds are heard from one
end of the world to the other, and these are: The sound
of the revolutions of the sun; the sound of the noise of
Rome, and the sound of the soul as it departs from the
body. Some say also the sound of birth. Some say also
of Ridya, the angel of rain. The Rabbis prayed for
mercy on the soul as it leaves the body, and so the sound
has stopped.

In accordance with Rabbi Shila it was stated: If one
starts on a journey before the cock crows, his blood is
upon his own head. Rabbi Josiah said: Not until he
has crowed a second time; and some say, till he has
crowed three times. What sort of a cock? They said,
an average cock.

Rab Yehuda said in the name of Rab: When the
Israelites gathered into the temple for the festivals they
stood tightly pressed, but when they prostrated them-

selves they did it in comfort. They extended eleven ells beyond the Holy of Holies—What does he mean by this? —He means as follows: Though they extended eleven ells beyond the Holy of Holies, when they stood tightly pressed, when they prostrated themselves they did it and there was plenty of space. This was one of the ten miracles that were performed in the Temple. . . .

(Gemara)

FROM CHAPTER I

NO MAN enters the Temple Court to do service until he immerses himself, even if he be clean. The High Priest immersed himself five times and made ten sanctifications of his hands and his feet on that day.

Between the Priest and the public there was spread a linen sheet. He took off his clothes, went down and immersed himself. He then came up and dried himself. They brought him gold garments, and he put them on, and sanctified his hands and his feet. They brought him the Daily-Offering. He made the incision in the neck while another priest finished the slaughtering. He received the blood and sprinkled it. He went in to burn the morning incense and to arrange the candles, and then to offer the head and the limbs, the pancakes, and the wine.

The morning incense was offered between the sprinkling of the blood and the offering of the limbs; that of the evening between the offering of the limbs and the Drink-Offering. If the High Priest was old or frail they used to prepare for him hot water. They poured it into the cold so as to take away the chill.

They brought him into the Parvah Chamber, which

belonged to the Holy ground. They spread a linen sheet between him and the public; he sanctified his hands and feet and took his garments off. Rabbi Meir says: He took off, sanctified his hands and feet, went down, immersed himself, came up and dried himself. They brought him white garments, he put them on and sanctified his hands and his feet.

In the morning he put on garments made of Pellusin linen worth twelve *minahs*. In the afternoon he wore clothes of India worth eight hundred *zuz*. This according to Rabbi Meir. But the Sages say: At dawn he put on garments worth eighteen *minahs* while in the afternoon his garments were worth twelve *minahs*. Altogether, thirty *minahs*. These were provided at the cost of the people, but if he wanted to spend more he could do so out of his own pocket.

He then went to his bullock. The bullock stood between the Hall and the Altar, its head was to the south and its face to the west. The Priest stood in the east and his face was to the west. He put his hands on the bullock and made his confession. And so he used to say: Oh, Lord, I have sinned; I have transgressed; I have committed iniquity before Thee. I and my house. O Lord, forgive the sins, the transgressions and the iniquities that I have sinned, transgressed and committed before Thee—I and my house, as it is written in the Laws of Moses, Thy servant: (*Lev.* xvi, 30) *For on that day shall the priest make an atonement for you, to cleanse you that ye may be clean from all your sins before the Lord.* And they answered after him: Blessed be the name of His glorious kingdom forever and ever.

He then came to the east, to the north of the Altar,

the deputy priest at his right, and the chief of the house of the Fathers of the Temple at his left. There were the two he-goats. There was also an urn with two straws, for drawing lots. They were made of boxwood, but ben Gamla later made them of gold, for which his name is remembered with praise.

BEN Katin made twelve corks for the washbasin that originally had only two. He also made a device for the basin, so that the water would not be contaminated during the night. King Monabaz made all the handles of the vessels of the day of Atonement out of gold. His mother, Helena, made a golden candelabra over the entrance to the Temple. She also made a tablet of gold, on which was written the paragraph of *Sotah*. A miracle happened to the gates of Nicanor, and he was remembered in honor.

But these were remembered in dishonor: Those of the House of Garmu—they would not teach how to make the Shew-bread; those of the house of Abtinas—for they would not teach how to make the incense; Hygros ben Levi, who knew how to sing, but would not teach it to anyone; Ben Kamtzar, who would not teach the art of writing. Of the first they said: (*Prov.* x, 7) *The memory of the just is blessed.* Of the latter it was said: (*Prov.* x, 7) *The name of the wicked shall rot.*

(*Gemara*)

"IN THE morning he put on garments made of Pellusin linen worth eighteen *minahs,* etc." Does the author wish to teach us anything by this? He teaches us that the sum total must not be changed, but one may spend

more on one and less on the other. But all are of the
opinion that the morning is more important than the
afternoon. Whence is this? Said Rabbi Huna ben
Elai: We read (*Lev.* xvi, 4) *Linen, linen, linen, linen.*
This means the best linen. An objection: (*Ezek.* xliv,
19) *And they shall put on other garments: and they shall
not sanctify the people with their garments.* "Others";
probably better than the ones?—No; "other" means in-
ferior ones.

WHEN the Public service is over, then a priest for
whom a mother made a garment may perform his personal offering in it, but after the service he should donate it to the community. Is not this self-evident? One
could think that perhaps the priest may not donate it to
the community. Therefore he teaches us thus: They related about Rabbi Ishmael ben Phabi that his mother
made him a garment worth a hundred *minahs.* He put
it on and performed the personal offering and then do-
nated it to the community. They said of Rabbi Eleazar
ben Harsom that his mother made for him a garment
worth two thousand *minahs,* but his brethren, the priests,
would not let him put it on for he looked in it as if he
were naked.—How could this be possible? Did not the
master say that the threads were six-ply?—Abaya answered: As transparent as the wine in a glass.

The Rabbis taught: The poor, the rich, and the evil
come before the Court of Heaven. They ask of the poor,
Why did you not occupy yourself with the study of the
law? If he says, I was poor and busy with my livelihood, they answered him: Were you poorer, then, than
Hillel? It was related about Hillel, the elder, that every

day he worked and earned a *tropaik*. Half of it he would give to the gate-keeper at the house of learning, and half was for his food and that of his household. One day he could not find his earnings, and the gate-keeper would not let him in. He hoisted himself up and sat on the window sill, so that he could hear the word of the living God from the lips of Shemaya and Abtalion. They say it was Sabbath eve in the fall of the year and snow came down upon him. When the dawn rose Shemaya said to Abtalion: Every day it is light in the house, while today it is dark. Is it a cloudy day? They looked up and saw the figure of a man in the window. They went up and found him covered with three cubits of snow. They brought him down, bathed him, rubbed him with oil and set him before the hearth. They said: He is worthy to have the Sabbath desecrated for his sake.

To a rich man they say: Why didn't you occupy yourself with the study of the Torah? If he says, I was rich and was busy with my possessions, they say to him: Were you richer than Rabbi Eleazar? They related of Rabbi Eleazar ben Harsom that his father left him a thousand villages on the mainland and a thousand ships on the oceans. But every day he would take a sack of flour on his shoulder and wander from town to town and from countryside to countryside in order to learn the *Torah*. One day his servants found him and drafted him for public work. He said to them: Please let me go, and let me study the law. Said they to him: By the life of Rabbi Eleazar ben Harsom, we shall not let you go. He never saw them again in his life, but all his life long he sat and studied the *Torah,* day and night.

To the wicked they say: Why didn't you occupy

yourself with the study of the Law? If he said: I was
handsome and because of my passion I had no time for
it, They would say to him: Were you, then, more handsome than Joseph? They said of Joseph, the righteous,
that every day the wife of Potiphar tried to lure him
with words. The clothes that she put on for his sake
in the morning, she would not wear in the evening. The
clothes that she wore in the evening, she would not wear
in the morning. She entreated him: "Listen to me", but
he said: "No." She said to him: "I shall put you in
prison." He said: (*Psalms* cxlvi, 7) *The Lord looseth
the prisoners.*—"I shall bend thy stature."—He answered: (*Psalms* cxlvi, 8) *The Lord raiseth them that
are bowed down.*— "I shall blind your eyes."— (*Ibid.*)
The Lord openeth the eyes of the blind. She then gave
him a thousand silver pieces, so that he should hearken
to her: (*Gen.* xxxix, 10) *to lie by her, or to be with her.*
But he would not submit to her, to lie with her in this
world, and to be with her in the world to come. In this
way Hillel condemns the poor, while Rabbi Eleazar ben
Harson condemns the rich, and Joseph condemns the
wicked.   (*Mishna*)

FROM CHAPTER III

HE SHOOK the urn and brought up two lots. On
one was written: "For the Lord," and on the other was
written: "To Azazel." The deputy was to his right,
and the Chief of the Fathers to his left. If the lot "For
the Lord" was in his right hand, the deputy priest would
say: My Master, High Priest, lift thy right hand; if
the lot "For the Lord" was in his left hand, the Father
of the House of the Temple would say: My Master, High

Priest, lift thy left hand. He put them on the two he-
goats, and said: "A Sin-offering for the Lord." Rabbi
Ishmael said: He does not have to say: "A Sin-Offering", but only "For the Lord," and they answered after
him: "Blessed be the Name of His glorious Kingdom
for ever and ever."

He bound a bright red wool ribbon on the head of
the scape-goat and turned it the way it would be sent out.
And the goat that was to be slaughtered he turned towards the place where it would be slaughtered. Then
he came again upon his bullocks, put his hands on them
and made his confession.   (*Mishna*)

FROM CHAPTER IV

THE ladle and the pan were handed to him. He took
two hands full of the incense and put it into the ladle,
which was large if his hand was large, and it was small
if his hand was small, for that was the measure. He
took the pan in his right hand and the ladle in his left
hand. He walked through the Temple till he came between the two curtains that separate the Holies from
the Holy of Holies. There was the space of an ell between them. Rabbi Yosi says, there was only one curtain, for it was said: (*Exodus* xxvi, 33) *And the veil
shall divide unto you between the holy place and the most
holy.* The outer curtain was tied back from the south
side, while the inner was tied back on the north side.
He walked between them until he reached the north side;
when he reachd the north he turned his face to the south,
and walkd to the left of the curtain, till he reached the
Ark. When he reached the Ark, he put the pan between
the two poles. He heaped up the incense on the coals,

and the whole house was filled with smoke. He went out the way he came in, and said a short prayer in the corridor. He did not prolong his prayer, so as not to terrify Israel.

When the Ark was taken away, there was a stone left there from the days of the early Prophets and it was called the "foundation stone"; it was three fingerbreadths high, and on this he put the pan.

He took the blood from the one who was stirring it. He entered the place where he was supposed to enter, and he stood in the place where he was supposed to stand, and sprinkled the blood once upwards and seven times downwards, he did not do it as though he were bent on sprinkling it upwards and downwards, but as though he were switching a whip, and he would count thus: One, one and one, one and two, one and three, one and four, one and five, one and six, and one and seven. Then he would go out and put it on the golden stand in the Temple. The he-goat was then brought to him. He slaughtered it, received the blood in a basin, and entered the place where he was supposed to enter. . . . Then he would come out and put it on the second golden stand. Rabbi Yehuda says: There was only one stand. He then took the blood of the bullock and then the blood of the he-goat and sprinkled it on the curtain outside, opposite the Ark, once upwards and seven times downwards, etc. He then poured the blood of the bullock into the blood of the he-goat and poured the full basin into the empty.

And he shall go out unto the Altar that is before the Lord (*Lev.* xvi, 18) This is the golden Altar. He began to sprinkle downwards. Where does he begin? From the north-east corner to the north-west, then south-west, then south-east, where he began the sin-offering on the outer Altar. Then he completed the sprinkling of the inner Altar. . . .

He then sprinkled over the clean part of the Altar seven times, and poured the rest of the blood at the western foundation of the outer Altar, and the blood remaining from the outer Altar he poured over the southern foundation. Both were mixed in the channel and then flowed out into the *Kidron,* and were sold to gardeners as fertilizer.

THE whole service of the Day of Atonement must be performed according to the order here related. If he perform one act before one that should precede it, it is void. If he sprinkle the blood of the he-goat before the blood of the bullock, he must go back and sprinkle the blood of the bullock before he sprinkles the blood of the he-goat. If the blood was poured out before he had finished the sprinkling in the inner Temple, he must get other blood and start anew: sprinkling first in the inner Temple, and so on, in the Temple, and on the golden Altar. For each of them is a separate atonement. Rabbi Eleazar and Rabbi Simon say: In the place where he stopped there he begins again.   (*Mishna*)

"AND said a short prayer." What did he pray for? Raba ben R. Ada and Rabin ben R. Ada both related in the name of Rab: "May it be Thy will, O Lord our God that the coming year be full of rains and hot"— Is then a hot year beneficial?—Rather he said: If it is hot, let there be plenty of rain. Rabbi Aha the son of Raba said the prayer according to Rabbi Yehuda: "May there not depart a ruler from the house of Judah. And may the People of Israel not require sustenance one of another. And hearken not to the prayers of travellers." Rabbi Hanina ben Dosa was travelling once, when a rain came down. He prayed: "Lord of the Universe, the whole world is comfortable, while I am suffering." The rain stopped at once. When he arrived home he said: "The whole world is suffering, while Hanina is comfortable." Immediately it began to rain. Rabbi Joseph said: Of what use is the prayer of the High Priest as against Rabbi Hanina ben Dosa?

The Rabbis said: There was once a High Priest who prolonged his prayer. His brethren the priests decided to go in and fetch him. They were about to enter when he came out. They said to him: Why have you prolonged your prayer? He answered: Is it so uncomfortable for you, that I prayed for you and for the Temple, that it may not be destroyed? Said they: You must not do so again, for we have learnt: "He did not prolong his prayer, so as not to terrify Israel." (*Gemara*)

FROM CHAPTER V

THE High Priest then came to read. If he wanted, he read wearing the linen garments; but if he wished, he could wear his own white cloak. The beadle of the synagogue would then take the scroll of the *Torah* and hand it to the Chief of the synagogue, the Chief of the synagogue would hand it to the deputy priest, and the deputy priest would hand it to the High Priest. The High Priest received it standing and read: (*Lev.* 16) *After the death* . . . and (*Lev.* xxiii, 27) *Also on the tenth day.* . . . Then he rolled up the scroll of the *Torah* and put it in his bosom and spoke: More than I have read before you is written here, *And on the tenth* which is in the *Book of Numbers,* he recited by heart. And he pronounced upon it eight benedictions: For the *Torah,* for the Service, for Thanksgiving, for the forgiveness of sin, and for the Temple separately, and for the People of Israel separately, and for Jerusalem separately, and for the priests separately, and for all others he said a prayer.

Who so saw the High Priest read, saw not the bullock and the he-goat being burnt. And he who saw the bullock and the he-goat burn, saw not the High Priest when he read. Not because this was forbidden, but because the distance was too great, and both acts were performed at the same time.

If he read in the linen garments, he sanctified his hands and his feet, took off his clothes, went down, immersed himself, came up and dried himself. Then his golden garments were brought to him, he put them on, sanctified his hands and his feet. Then he went out and performed his Ram Offering, and the Ram Offering for the people, and the seven young lambs. Thus according to Rabbi Eliezer. Rabbi Akiba says: These were offered with the morning Daily-Offering. While the bullock for the Whole-Offering, and the he-goat that are offered outside, were offered with the Daily-Offering of the afternoon.

He then sanctified his hands and feet, went down, immersed himself, came up and dried himself. The white linen garments were brought to him, he put them on and again sanctified his hands and feet. He then went in to get the ladle and the pan. He sanctified his

hands and his feet, took off his garments, went down,
immersed himself, came up, dried himself.   His golden
garments were brought to him, he put them on, sanctified his hands and his feet, and went in to burn the
afternoon incense and to fix the candles.   Again he sanctified his hands and his feet, and took the garments off.
His own clothes were then brought to him; he then
dressed; and they accompanied him to his home.   And
he was wont to prepare a feast for his friends, because
he had returned safely from the Temple.

The High Priest performs the service in eight vest-
ments, while the ordinary priest performs in four;—in a
robe, trousers, a mitre and a girdle.   The High Priest
adds a breast plate, an apron, a cloak, and a frontlet; in
these were the *Urim* and *Thummim* of which inquiries
were made.   But they inquired only for the King, or for
the Chief of the Court, or for one who was indispensable
to the community.   (*Mishna*)

FROM CHAPTER VII

ON THE Day of Atonement it is forbidden to eat,
drink, wash, anoint, put on sandals, and to have marital
relations.   The King and the bride may wash their faces
and a woman who is just after childbirth may put on her
sandals.   Thus according to Rabbi Eliezer, but the Sages
forbid it.   (*Mishna*)

THE Rabbis taught: (*Lev.* vii, 23) *Ye shall afflict
your souls.*   One may think that he must sit in the sun
or in a cold place so that he shall cause suffering to himself.   Therefore we learned (*Lev.* xvi, 29) *And ye shall
do no manner of work.*   Just as no work means: sit and

do nothing, so does affliction mean: sit and do nothing—
Perhaps this means that if one is sitting in the sun, and
is hot he must not change his place and sit down in the
shade, or if he is sitting in the shade and is cold; he must
not sit down in the sun?—Just as with work: Just as we
make no distinction between work and work, so there is
no distinction between affliction.

*Who fed in the wilderness with Manna . . . that he
might humble thee* (*Deut.* viii, 16). Rabbi Ammi and
Rabbi Assi are discoursing. One says: One that has a
piece of bread in his basket cannot be likened to one who
has no bread in his basket. The other said: One that eats
and sees what he eats cannot be likened to one who eats
and cannot see what he is eating. Said Rabbi Joseph:
This refers to the blind who eat and are never fully satisfied. Said Abaya: If one possesses only one meal he
should eat during the daytime. Rabbi Zera said: Which
verse refers to this? (*Eccl.* vi, 9) *Better is the sight of
the eyes than the wandering of the desire.* Resh Lakish
said: It is more pleasant to look at a woman than the
act itself, for it was said: *Better is the sight of the eyes
than the wandering of the desire.*

*When it giveth his colour in the cup, when it moveth
itself aright.* (*Prov.* xxiii, 31.) Rabbi Ammi and Rabbi
Assi are discoursing. One says: When a man fixes his
eye on the cup, all incest laws are as smooth as a plain
to him. The other says: A man who fixes his eye on the
cup, the whole world appears to him like a plain.

Heaviness in the heart of man maketh it stoop.
(*Prov.* xii, 25.) Rabbi Ammi and Rabbi Assi. One
says: One should take it off his mind. The other says:
One should tell it to another.

And dust shall be the serpent's meat. (*Isaiah* lxv,
25.) Rabbi Ammi and Rabbi Assi. One says: If the
serpent would eat the finest delicacies of the world, he
would taste in them the taste of earth. The other says:
If he ate all the finest delicacies in the world, he would not
be satisfied until he had eaten earth.

Said Rabbi Yosi: Come and see, how different are
the methods of the Lord, blessed be He, from those of
flesh and blood. If one of flesh and blood becomes angry
at his neighbour, he annoys him to death, but the Holy
One, blessed be He, is not like that. He cursed the serpent, but if the serpent goes up to the roof it finds its
food there; if it comes down, its food is there, too.
He cursed Canaan, but he eats what his master is eating,
and he drinks whatever his master is drinking. He
cursed the woman, but everyone is running after her.
He cursed the earth, but everyone is being nourished
from it. (*Gemara*)

SMALL children are not permitted to fast on the Day
of Atonement. But they should be initiated a year or
two before they become of age, so that they may become
used to fulfilling the precepts.

If a pregnant woman smelled food, she should be
given to eat till she is satisfied. One that is sick should
be given food at the advice of an expert person. But
if there is no expert, one gives him food if he wishes it,
until he says: "Enough".

If one is overcome because of hunger he may be given
even unclean food to eat, till his eyes lighten up. If a
mad dog has bitten one, he may not be given the lobe of
its liver to eat, but Rabbi Matithiah ben Heresh permits

it. And furthermore Rabbi Matithiah ben Heresh said:
If one has a sore throat, they may drop medicine into his
mouth, because this may be a matter of life and death.
And in a matter of life and death, Sabbath is overridden.

(*Mishna*)

IF A pregnant woman smelt holy meat or the meat of
a swine, one puts a spindle in the broth and places it on
her mouth. If this satisfies her it is well; if not, one
lets her eat the broth; if that satisfied her it is well; if
not, one gives her some fat meat because there is nothing that may stand in the way of saving a life except
idolatry, incest, or bloodshed. Whereof do we know of
idolatry? For it was taught: Rabbi Eliezer said: It was
written: (*Deut.* vi, 5) *With all thy soul.* Why was it
said: (*ibid*) *With all thy might?* And if it was said:
With all thy might, why was it said: *With all thy soul?*
This was said for a person to whom his life is dearer
than his gold, therefore it was said: *With all thy soul.*
But in case there is a man to whom his gold is dearer to
him than his life, it was said: *With all thy might.*

Whereof do we know of incest and bloodshed?—We
learned: Rabbi said: (*Deut.* xxii, 26) *For when a man
riseth against his neighbor, and slayeth him, even so is
this matter.* Why this comparison between bloodshed
and the rage of a betrothed maiden? This was meant
to teach us, and indeed it does teach: Just as we are obligated to save the betrothed maiden even if we have to
kill the man that is trying to rape her, so is it also in
the case of a murderer. And just as we should rather
be killed than murder another person, so also in the case
of a betrothed maiden, one should rather allow himself

to be killed than commit rape. But wherefrom do we deduce that this applies to murder?—This is simple. A man came once to Raba and said to him: The Chief of my village instructed me to kill some one. He said, if I do not kill the man, he will kill me. Raba answered: Let him kill you; but you must not commit murder. Do you believe that your blood is redder than his? The blood of that man may be redder than yours.

Once a pregnant woman smelt food. They inquired of Rabbi. He said: Go and whisper into her ear that this is the Day of Atonement. They did it, and she was quite satisfied. Whereupon Rabbi proclaimed this verse: (*Jeremiah* i, 5) *Before I formed thee in the belly I knew thee.* Her offspring was Rabbi Yohanan.

Then there was the case of another pregnant woman who smelt food; when they inquired of Rabbi Hanina, he too said: Go and whisper into her ear that this is the Day of Atonement. They did it, but she was not satisfied. The Rabbi then pronounced the verse: (*Psalms* lviii, 3) *The wicked are estranged from the womb.* Her offspring was Shabbatai, the hoarder of provisions.

(*Gemara*)

IF SOMEONE is caught beneath a fallen structure, and there is doubt whether he is there or not, whether he is alive or dead, whether he is a Jew or a Gentile, they must clear away the debris. If the man is found alive they may continue the clearing, but if he is dead, they must leave him there.   (*Mishna*)

IF ONE is overcome with hunger he should be given honey and all sorts of sweets, for honey and sweet food enlighten the eyes; though there is no proof of this, there is an intimation of it, for it was said: (1 *Samuel* xiv, 29) *See, I pray you how mine eyes have been enlightened, because I tasted a little of this honey.* Why is this no proof?—Because here there are no words of being overcome with hunger. Abaya said: This refers only to eating after the meal; but before the meal such things stimulate the appetite, for it is written: (1 *Samuel* xxxii, 12) *And they found an Egyptian in the field and brought him to David, and gave him bread, and he did eat; and they made him drink water. And they gave him a piece of a cake of figs, and two clusters of raisins; and when he had eaten, his spirit came again to him; for he had eaten no bread, nor drunk any water, three days and three nights.*

Rab Nahman said in the name of Samuel: If one is overcome with hunger, he should be given a piece of fat tail-meat with honey. Rab Huna ben Rabbi Joshua said: Also pure flour with honey. Rab Papa said: Even barley flour with honey. Rabbi Yohanan said: I was once overcome by hunger. I ran to the eastern side of a fig tree, and thus have myself fulfilled the verse: (*Eccl.* vii, 12) *Wisdom giveth life to them that have it.* For Rab Joseph taught: If one wants to experience the real taste of a fig, he should turn to the eastern side, for it was said: (*Deut.* xxxiii, 14) *And for the precious fruits brought forth by the sun.*

Rabbi Yehuda and Rabbi Yosi were walking once, when Rabbi Yehuda was suddenly overcome by hunger. He overpowered a shepherd and ate his bread. Rabbi Yosi said to him: You have robbed a shepherd. When they arrived at the town, Rabbi Yosi was seized by a ravenous hunger. They brought before him all kinds of foods and dishes. Then said Rabbi Yehuda to him: I robbed only one shepherd but you have robbed a whole city.

RABBI Meir, Rabbi Yehuda and Rabbi Yosi were once on a journey. Rabbi Meir was always particular about the names of people, but Rabbi Yehuda and Rabbi Yosi never bothered about them. They once came to some place and looked for lodgings, which they found. They asked the innkeeper what was his name and he said: Kidor. Then said Rabbi Meir, I gather that he is an evil man, for it was said: (*Deut.* xxxii, 20) *For they are a very forward generation (Kidor).* Rabbi Yehuda and Rabbi Yosi entrusted to him their money, but Rabbi Meir did not. He hid it in the grave of that man's father. The innkeeper dreamed that some one said to him: Go and take the purse that is lying under that man's head. The next morning he told them about his dream. Said they to him: A dream of a Sabbath night has no meaning. Thereupon Rabbi Meir waited the whole day and took away his purse. The next morning they said to the innkeeper: Give us our purses. He answered that he knew nothing about them. Then Rabbi Meir said to them: Why didn't you pay any attention to the name? They answered:—Why didn't you call our attention to it, Master? He replied: I considered that one ought to be suspicious, but I did not consider it a certainty. Thereupon they asked the innkeeper to go with them to a shop where they noticed lentils in his beard. Whereupon they went to his wife and gave her this as a sign that he had ordered them to return the purses, and they received their purses. When he returned home he killed his wife. This

is whereby we learned about the washing of hands after
the meal, the second water, which causes one to commit
murder. From then on they too paid attention to names.
Once they came to the house of a man named Balah, they
did not enter the house, for they said: He must be an
evil man, for it is written: (*Ezek.* xxiii, 43) *Then said
I unto her that was old in adulteries* (*Balah*).

THE Rabbis taught: A life must be saved on the Sabbath, and the faster one goes about it the more praiseworthy he is; he does not need the permission of the
Court for it. If one saw a child fall into the water, he
should spread a net and pull it out; the faster the more
praiseworthy, and he needs no permission of the Court
to do it, even though he should catch fish while doing it.
If a child fell into a pit one may tear out a joint and pull
it up; the quicker he does it the better, and he needs no
permission of the Court for it, even though by doing it
he builds a stair. If one sees a door closing upon a child
he may chop it down in order to get the child out quickly;
and the faster he does the more praiseworthy he is, and
he needs no permission of the Court for it, though by
doing this he deliberately splits the wood. One extin-
guishes and isolates a fire during a conflagration on the
Sabbath; and the faster one works the more praiseworthy
he is, and he needs no permission of the Court for it,
though while performing this he deliberately makes charcoal.—And all these cases are mentioned advisedly, for
if it were spoken only of the case of a child falling into
the water one would think it was only because the water
may carry away the child, but it does not apply to a
child that falls into a pit. For the child may remain in

the pit till the man obtain permission from the court.
Therefore this case is mentioned too. But since one
might say that in this case it is permitted because the
child may be terrified, therefore the case of the door is
mentioned, because one could sit on the other side of the
door and amuse the child by making a noise with nuts.
But why is the instance of the fire and isolation mentioned? —This is to indicate that it also applies to a fire
in the court of a neighbor.   (*Gemara*)

SIN-OFFERING and Guilt-Offering bring forgiveness
for certain transgressions. Death and the Day of Atonement bring forgiveness, if there is repentance. Repentance brings forgiveness for light transgressions. Positive and negative commandments and severe transgressions must wait till their forgiveness is brought about
on the Day of Atonement. If one says: I will sin and
repent, sin and repent, he is not given the opportunity
to repent. If he says: I will sin and the Day of Atonement will bring about my forgiveness—he is not forgiven
on the Day of Atonement. Sins that are committed
against Heaven, the Day of Atonement brings their forgiveness, but sins committed as between one person and
another, the Day of Atonement does not bring their forgiveness until the person sinned against grants his forgiveness. This was explained by Rabbi Eleazar ben
Azariah: (*Lev.* xvi, 30) *That you may be clean from all
your sins before the Lord.*

Rabbi Akiba said: Fortunate are the people of Israel.
Before whom do you become clean, and who cleanses
you? Your Father, Who is in Heaven, for it was said:
(*Ezek.* xxxvi, 25) *Then I will sprinkle clean water upon*

you and ye shall be clean.   And it also says: (*Jeremiah*
xvii, 13) *O Lord, the hope of Israel.*   Just as the fountain of waters purifies the unclean, so will the Holy One,
blessed be His name, cleanse the House of Israel.

(*Mishna*)

FROM CHAPTER VIII

Days of Fasting

(Tractate Taanith)

RABBI Yohanan said: There are three keys which the Holy One, blessed be He, has not entrusted into the hands of any messenger, but keeps in his own hand. These are: The key of rain, the key of birth, and the key of the resurrection of the dead. The key of rain, for it is written: (*Deut.* xxviii, 12) *The Lord shall open unto thee his good treasure, the heaven to give the rain unto the land in his season.* The key of birth, for it is written: (*Gen.* xxx, 22) *And God remembered Rachel, and God hearkened to her, and opened her womb.* The key of the resurrection of the dead, for it is written: (*Ezek.* xxxvii, 13) *And ye shall know that I am the Lord, when I have opened your graves.* In the West they said, also the key of sustenance, for it is written: (*Psalms* cxlv, 16) *Thou openest thy hand, etc.* Why did not Rabbi Yohanan include this?—Well, he can say that "Rains" includes sustenance also.

It was taught: The clouds and the winds are only secondary to the rain. Which ones are they? Ulla, and

131

some say it was Rab Yehuda, said: Those that follow
the rain, are these then beneficial? Is it not written:
(*Deut.* xxviii, 24) *The Lord shall make the rain of thy
land powder and dust.* To this Ulla, and some say it
was Rabbi Yehuda, said: Does this mean the wind that
comes after the rain?—There is no contradiction here.
One speaks of a gentle rain, while the other means a
downpour. This latter throws up dust, while the first
does not.

Further Rabbi Yehuda said: The wind that comes
after the rain is as good as the rain; clouds that come
after the rain are as good as the rain; sunshine after the
rain is doubly beneficial. What is excluded here? The
glow of the evening and sunshine between the clouds.

Raba said: Snow is as beneficial to the mountain as
five-fold rain to the earth, for it was said: (*Job* xxxvii,
6) *For he saith to the snow, Be thou on the earth, likewise to the small rain, and to the great rain of his
strength.* And Raba also said: Snow for the mountains,
hard rain for the trees, a gentle rain for fruit of the
fields, and even a drizzle is good for the seeds under the
hard sod.

Further Raba said: A young scholar is like a seed
under the hard sod; if he begins to sprout, he will shoot
forth. Raba also said: If a young scholar falls into a
rage, it is only because the *Torah* has enraged him, for
it was said: (*Jeremiah* xxiii, 29) *Is not my word like as
a fire? saith the Lord.*   (*Gemara*)

IF ON the seventeenth of Marheshwan no rain has
as yet fallen, then some individuals begin to fast three
days. They eat and drink after sundown, they may

work, wash themselves, anoint themselves, put on sandals, and they may have marital relations. If the first
of Kislev came and no rain has fallen, the court then
orders the public to fast three days; they may eat and
drink after sundown. They may work, wash themselves,
anoint themselves, put on sandals, and they may have
marital relations.   (*Mishna*)

THE Rabbis taught: When the people of Israel find
themselves in trouble, and one of them separates himself from the people, then the two angels of service, who
accompany every person, come and lay their hands on
his head and say: So-and-so, who has separated himself
from the people, shall not see the consolation of the people. In another place we learned: When the people find
themselves in trouble, let not a man say, I will go into
my home and eat and drink, and all will be well with
me. If he does so, it is of him that was written: (*Isaiah
xxii, 13*) *And behold joy and gladness, slaying oxen,
and killing sheep, eating flesh, and drinking wine: let us
eat and drink for tomorrow we shall die. . . .* A man
should share in the sorrows and troubles of his community, for thus we found our master Moses, that he shared
in common with the community its sorrows and troubles,
for it was said: (*Exodus xvii, 12*) *But Moses' hands
were heavy, and they took a stone, and put it under him
and he sat thereon.* Did not Moses have a cushion or a
bolster to sit upon? This is to teach us that Moses
wished to say: "All of Israel find themselves in trouble,
I too will suffer with them." And every person who
shares in the sorrows of the community, lives to see also
the consolation of the community. And perchance there

will be one who will say: "Who is there that will testify against me?"—The stones of one's own house and the beams of his roof testify against him, for it was said: (*Habakkuk* ii, 11) *For the stone shall cry out of the wall, and the beam out of the timber shall answer it.* In the school of Rabbi Shila it was said that the two angels of service who accompany each person will testify against him, for it was said: (*Psalms* xci, 11) *For he shall give his angels charge over thee.* Rabbi Hidka said: A man's own soul testifies against him, for it was said: (*Micah* vii, 5) *Keep the doors of thy mouth from her that lieth in thy bosom.*   (*Gemara*)

IF THESE days passed and rain had not fallen, the court orders the community to fast another three days. They may eat and drink while it is still day, but they are not permitted to work, to wash themselves, to anoint themselves, to put on sandals, nor to have marital relations; and the bathhouses must be kept closed. If these days passed and rain had not come, the court orders a further fast of seven days, making it thirteen all together. These surpass the first day, for on these days they blow the horn and they close the shops. On Mondays they are permitted to open the shops partially, but on the fifth day they are permitted to open the shops because of the honor of the Sabbath. If these days passed, and no rains had fallen, men refrain from their business affairs, they also refrain from building, and from planting; no betrothals or marriages are arranged, and people do not greet one another, as should be with men who have merited the scorn of the Lord. Certain individuals fast till the end of Nisan. If the rains came after Nisan has passed, it is a sign of a curse, for it was said: (1 *Samuel* xii, 17) *Is it not wheat harvest today?* etc. . . .   (*Mishna*)

IT IS logical that they would forbid the pleasures of bathing, anointing and intercourse; but why forbid work that is drudgery? Rabbi Hisda answered, in the name of Rabbi Jeremiah ben Abba: The *Scriptures* say: (*Joel* i, 14) *Sanctify ye a fast, call a solemn assembly, gather the elders.* This means that a fast day is as a solemn assembly; just as one is not permitted to work during a solemn assembly, so one must not work on a fast day. . . .
                                               (*Gemara*)
                                  FROM CHAPTER I

WHAT is the ritual of the days of fasting? They take out the Ark into the public place in the town, they put wood ashes on the Ark, on the head of the Prince and on the head of the Chief Justice of the Court, and everyone puts ashes on his own head. The eldest among them recites before them words of admonition: "My brethren, it was not said of the people of Nineveh that the Lord saw their sackcloth and their fasting, but (*Jonah* iii, 10) *And God saw their works, that they turned from their evil ways* and it is further said: (*Joel* ii, 13) *Rend your heart and not your garments.*"

They stood in prayer, and they sent down to the Ark an old man who knew how to recite the prayers, a man who had children, and who was in want, so that his heart would be filled with his prayers. He would recite before them twenty-four benedictions, the eighteen of the daily ritual, and he would add six more.

During the first three days of fasting the priests on duty would fast, but not throughout the day; but the priests of the House of Fathers did not fast at all. On the second three days, the priests on duty would fast throughout the whole day, while the priests of the House of Fathers would fast part of the day. On the last seven days they all fasted throughout the whole of the day. These are the words of Rabbi Joshua, but the Sages say: On the first three days none of the priests were fasting, on the second three days, the priests on watch duty fasted part of the day, but the priests of the House of the Fathers did not fast at all. On the last seven days, the priests of the watch fasted throughout the day while the priests of the House of the Fathers fasted, but only part of the day.

A public fast must not be ordered to begin on a Thursday, so as not to disrupt the prices in the market; but they order a three day fast to begin Monday to be followed by fasting again Thursday and then Monday.

(*Mishna*)

FROM CHAPTER II

IF THERE is an epidemic of pestilence in a city, or houses collapse in it, that city fasts and causes the sounding of horns, and in all the surrounding places they fast, but do not sound the horn. Rabbi Akiba says: they sound the horn, but they do not fast. What is termed an epidemic? If in a city that can furnish five hundred infantry men three deaths occur there in three consecutive days, it may be defined as a city in which an epidemic rages. If it is less than this, then there is no epidemic.

On the following occasions the horn is sounded: A

blight; mildew; locusts; crickets; wild beasts; and the danger of the sword of an enemy. They sound the horn because this is a spreading calamity.

It happened that the Sages went down from Jerusalem to their own towns and ordered a fast because a blight the size of an oven's mouth was seen in Ashkelon. And they also ordered a fast because wolves devoured two children on the other side of the Jordan. Rabbi Yosi said not because they devoured the children, but because they were seen.

For the following they sound the horn on the Sabbath: If a city is surrounded by an enemy, if it is flooded by a river, or if a ship is sinking in the harbor. Rabbi Yosi says: They sound the horn to summon help, but not as a call to God. Simon the Yemenite said: They also sound the horn in the case of pestilence, but the Sages did not agree with him.

They sound the horn for any affliction that befalls the public, excepting for an oversupply of rain.

It happened once that they said to Honi the circle-maker: "Pray for rain to fall." He replied, go and fetch the Passover-ovens from the open so they won't dissolve. He prayed but the rains did not come. What did he do? He made a circle and stood within, and said: Lord of the Universe, thy children have turned to me for I am as one of Thy household. I swear by Thy great name that I shall not move from my place till Thou hast compassion upon Thy children. Then rain began to fall in small drops. Then he said: Not for that sort of rain did I pray, but for rain to fill cisterns, pits and caves. Then rain began to fall in great violence. Whereupon

he said: Not for this sort of rain did I pray, but for a
rain of good will, of benevolence and bounty. Then rain
began to fall in the usual way, and it rained till the people of Israel had to leave Jerusalem and go up to the
Mount of the Temple. Then they came to Honi and
said to him: As thou has prayed for the rain to come,
go now and pray for the rain to leave us. He said to
them: Go and see if the stone of the Strayers has been
washed away. Simon ben Shetah sent word to him:
"Hadst thou not been Honi, I would have declared a
Ban against thee. But what shall I do to thee? Thou
petitionest the Lord and He does as thou askest him, as
if thou wert a son who petitions a father, and the father
fulfills his will. It is of thy kind that it was written:
(*Proverbs* xxiii, 25) *Thy father and thy mother shall be
glad, and she that bare thee shall rejoice.*"   (*Mishna*)

WHAT is a plague of drought?—Rab Yehuda said
in the name of Rab: A plague which causes drought.
Rab Nahman said: When to a field that is situated on a
stream we have to bring water from another stream,
then we call it drought. But when it has to be brought
from another land, then it is a famine. Rabbi Hanina
said: If one *seah* of grain costs a *sela,* but it is not to be
had, then it is called famine. Rabbi Yohanan said: This
is spoken only of the time when money is cheap, but produce is dear, but when money is dear while produce is
cheap, then they sound the horn forthwith. For Rabbi
Yohanan said: I remember distinctly a time when four
seah of grain cost only one *sela,* but people in Tiberias
were swelling from hunger, because there was not an
issar to be had.

Rabbi Eleazar ben Perata said: From the day that the Temple was destroyed the rainfalls were reduced. In some years there was plenty of rainfall, while in other years there was little. In some years the rain came in season, while in other years it came out of season. The year in which the rains came in season is to be compared to a servant to whom the master gave the food allowance on the first day of the week. Then we find that the dough is baked well and can be eaten with satisfaction. The year in which rains came out of season is compared to a servant to whom the master gave the allowance on the eve of Sabbath; we then find that the dough is not baked well. The year in which rain is plentiful is compared to a servant to whom the master gave the whole yearly allowance at one time, so that in the mill the loss in the grinding of a *kor* is the same as the loss in grinding of a *kab* and in the kneading the same waste entails in the kneading of a *kor* as in kneading a *kab*. A year in which the fall of rain is small may be compared to the servant to whom the master gives the allowance in small doses, we then find in the mill the loss in grinding a *kab* the same as that in a *kor,* and likewise the waste in kneading a *kab* is the same as that in a *kor*. Another comparison: When the rainfall is plentiful it may be compared to a man who kneads clay. If he has plenty of water, he does not use up all of it and the clay is well kneaded, but if he has little water, he will use up all that he has and the clay will not be kneaded properly.

THE Rabbis taught: Once the Israelites came for the pilgrimage to Jerusalem, and there was no water for drinking purposes. Nakdimon ben Gurion went to a

heathen magnate and said to him: Lend me twelve reser-
voirs of water for which I will return to you twelve wells
of water, or if I fail to give you the wells, I shall give
you twelve silver pieces, and he set a time limit for the
return of the payment. When the day of repayment
came, and rain had not fallen, the magnate sent word to
Nakdimon that morning: "Return to me the water or
the money that I have with you," but Nakdimon replied:
"I have time the whole day." At midday he again received
word to return the water or the money. Nakdimon replied: "I still have time to-day." Toward sundown again
he received the message: "Return to me the water or the
money that I have with you." But Nakdimon replied:
"I still have time till the day is over." Whereupon the
magnate sneered at him. He said: "Now that rains had
not fallen the whole year, you expect them to fall now?"
and in a cheerful mood he went down to the baths. Nakdimon went to the temple very depressed. He covered
himself with his shawl and prayed before the Lord. He
said: "Lord of the Universe. It is revealed and known
to Thee that I have not done this for my glory and not
for the glory of my father's house, but I have done this
for Thy glory so that the pilgrims shall have water for
drinking." At once the skies were darkened with clouds,
and rain fell so that the twelve wells were filled with
water and there was even an overflow. When the magnate was coming out of the bath-house, Nakdimon was
emerging from the Temple. When they met Nakdimon
said to the magnate: "Pay me for the overflow that I
have with you." This one answered him: "I know that
the Holy One, blessed be He, disturbed the world only
for your sake, but I still have a claim against you, for

the sun had already set, therefore the rains fell when
the matter was already out of your hands." Nakdimon
then returned to the Temple, covered himself with his
shawl and stood in prayer and said: "Lord of the Universe! Make known that thou hast beloved ones in Thy
world." At once the clouds were dispersed and the sun
shone again.

*FOR the Lord shall smite Israel, as a reed is shaken
in the water* (1 *Kings* xiv, 15). Rab Yehuda said in
the name of Rab: This is a blessing. For Rabbi Samuel
ben Nahmani said in the name of Rabbi Yohanan: Why
is it written: (*Proverbs* xxvii, 6) *Faithful are the
wounds of a friend; but the kisses of an enemy are deceitful.* Better is the curse of Ahiyah the Shilonite with
which he cursed the people of Israel, than the blessing
with which the wicked Balaam blessed them. Ahiyah
the Shilonite cursed them by comparing them to a reed,
he said to Israel: *For the Lord shall smite, etc.* As the
reed grows by the water, its stem grows new shoots and
its roots are many, and though all the wind of the universe blow upon it, they cannot move it from its place,
for it bends with the wind; if the winds stop, it goes back
to its upright position. But the wicked Balaam blessed
them by comparing them to the cedar, as it was said:
(*Numbers* xxiv, 6) *As cedar trees beside the waters.*
Now, the cedar does not grow by the water and its stock
does not bring forth new shoots and its roots are not
many, and all the winds in the universe cannot move it
from its place. However if a south wind should blow at
it, it uproots and turns it over. And not this alone, but
the reed was honored so that pens are made of it for

the writing of the Law, the Prophets and Hagiographa.

THE Rabbis taught: A man should always be as ten-
der as the reed, and he should not be as hard as the
cedar. It happened once that Rabbi Eleazar ben Simon
was coming from Migdal Gedor, from the home of his
teacher. He was riding an ass, sauntering on the banks
of a river. He was very happy and in an elated mood,
for he had done well in his studies. He met a man who
was very ugly. The man greeted him: "Peace be with
you, Master", but he did not return the greeting to him,
but said instead: How ugly you are. Are all your towns-
people as ugly as you are? The man replied: I do not
know, but go and tell my Maker and say to him: "How
ugly is the vessel which thou hast made." Rabbi Eleazar
realized at once that he had sinned, he dismounted from
his ass and prostrated himself before the man and said
to him: "I beseech you to forgive me." The man replied: I will not forgive you till you have gone to the
Master that created me and say to him: How ugly is
the vessel that thou hast made. Rabbi Eleazar walked
behind him till they arrived at the city. Here the towns-
people came out and said to him: Peace be with you, our
teacher, our master. The man said to them: Whom are
you addressing as our teacher, our master? They answered: The one that is walking behind you. Whereupon he said to them: If this is our teacher, then may
there be no more like him in Israel. They asked him
what was the reason, and he told them: "So-and-so he
did to me." Just the same, they said to him, you must
forgive him, because he is truly a great man and a great
scholar. He then replied: For your sake I shall forgive

him, with the understanding that he shall never do the
like again.

SAID Raba to Rabbi Rafrom ben Papa: Will the
master, kindly, tell us some of the good deeds that Rab
Huna was in the habit of doing? He answered: I do not
remember much of his childhood days, but well do I remember the deeds of his later life. On cloudy days he
would be driven in a golden carriage and he would inspect the whole city. He would have every weak wall
pulled down. If the owner was able to rebuild it, he
would do so; otherwise Rab Huna would rebuild it for
him at his own expense. On every Sabbath eve, he
would send his servant into the market place, who would
there buy off all the vegetables that remained in the hands
of the gardeners and would have them thrown into the
river.—Why? He could have given them away to the
poor.—The poor would then come to rely upon him, and
would not buy anything in the market.—Well, he could
have given them to some animals.—He was of the opinion that food which was fit for humans should not be
given to animals.—Then he should not have bought them
up.—Then the gardeners would not bring enough into
the market.

When he had some good medicine he would fill a jar
with it and suspend it above his door, and would announce: Whoever may have need of it let him come and
help himself. Some say he knew of a cure for *sibetha*
and he suspended a jar full of water and announced:
Whoever suffers from *sibetha*, let him come and wash
his hands with it and save his life thereby. Whenever
he was at meal, he would open his door and announce:

Whoever wishes let him come in and partake of my meal. Rabba said: I could do all these things myself, except the last one, because there are too many people in Mahuza.

Ilfa and Rabbi Yohanan studied the Law together, and they were both very poor. They once talked it over and decided that they would engage in business and fulfill the text: (*Deut.* xv, 4) *Save when there shall be no poor among you.* Then they sat down against a weak wall and ate their meal. Then two angels came, and Rabbi Yohanan heard one of them say: Let's throw the wall over upon these two men and kill them, for they forsook the eternal for things earthly. However, one of the angels said: No, leave them alone, for one of them has a great future before him. Whereupon Yohanan said to Ilfa: Master, have you heard anything? but Ilfa answered: No. Rabbi Yohanan thought: Since I heard it and Ilfa did not, it must be I who am destined to do great things. He then said to Ilfa: I will go back and fulfill the verse: (*Deut.* xv, 11) *For the poor shall never cease out of the land.* Whereupon Rabbi Yohanan was installed as rector of the Academy, and the scholars said to Ilfa: Had you remained here to study, you would have been rector of the Academy.

IT IS related of Nahum of Gamzu that he was totally blind, that both of his arms and legs were amputated, and his whole body was covered with boils. He was lying in a dilapidated house, and the legs of his bed were standing in basins of water, so that the ants would not crawl up on him. His disciples came to take him out from the house, and then they intended to take out his things. Whereupon he said to them: take the things out first, and then take me out in my bed, for I assure you as long as I am in it the house will not collapse, but as soon as you take me out, the house is sure to collapse. They took the things out first and then they took him out in his bed. No sooner was he out than the house collapsed. His disciples said to him: Master, since you are so wholly righteous, why should all this have happened to you? He answered then: My children, I brought it all upon myself. Once, on a journey to the house of my father-in-law, I had with me three asses, one laden with food, one with liquids, and one with costly delectables. A poor man came upon me on the road and stopped me and said to me: Master, give me some food: I replied, Wait till I unload one of the asses. Before I had time to unload the ass, the man expired. I fell upon the man and exclaimed: My eyes that have had no pity upon you shall be blinded, my arms that had no pity upon your arms shall fall off, and my legs that had no pity upon your legs shall be cut off. I was not satisfied till I said: My whole body shall be covered with sores. His disciples cried: Woe to us that we see you in such a state. He replied, It would have been woe to me had you not seen me in such a state. Why was he called Nahum Gamzu? Because whatever happened to him he would say: this too (gam-zu) is for the best.

Once the Israelites wished to send gifts to Caesar. After a consultation they decided to send Nahum of Gamzu, because so many miracles had happened to him. They entrusted into his hand a chest full of precious stones and pearls: He then started on his journey; but

when he stayed overnight in one of the inns, robbers
came and pilfered his chest and filled it with earth. The
next day when Nahum discovered the loss, he said: This
too is for the best. When he arrived at the palace, the
king wanted to kill him and all his men, for he said:
The Jews are jesting with me. Nahum, however, said:
This too is for the best. Then Elijah appeared, disguised as one of them, and said: Perhaps this is some
of the earth of their father Abraham, which turns into
swords when it is thrown against the enemy, for it is
written: (*Isaiah* xli, 2) *He gave them as the dust to
his sword, and as driven stubble to his bow.* They tried
it against the enemy of a province that could not be conquered, but with the earth it was conquered this time.
Whereupon they brought Nahum into the palace, filled
his chest full of precious stones and pearls, and sent him
home full of honors. On his return trip, when he stopped
again at the same inn he was asked: What did you bring
to the Emperor, that you were sent back with such great
honor? He answered: The things that I had taken with
me from here. The people of the inn then razed their
house to the ground, and took the earth to Caesar and
said to him. The earth which that man brought you
was ours. They tested it and found it was worthless.
Whereupon they put the innkeeper and his men to death.

(*Gemara*)

FROM CHAPTER III

FIVE things befell our ancestors on the seventeenth
of Tamuz, and five on the ninth of Ab. On the seventeenth of Tamuz the Tablets were broken, and the Daily-
Offering ceased, and the city was taken by assault, and

Apostomus burned the *Torah,* and he put an image into
the Temple. On the ninth of Ab it was decreed that
our ancestors be forbidden from entering the Land of
Israel, and the Temple was destroyed for the first and
also for the second time, and the City of Bethar was conquered, and the city was ploughed up. When the month
of Ab comes in, happiness should disappear.

RABBI Simon ben Gamaliel said: There were no better days in Israel then the fifteenth of Ab and the Day
of Atonement, for on them the daughters of Jerusalem
would go out in white garments that were borrowed,
so as not to shame those that had none of their own.
All the garments had to be washed first. And the daughters of Jerusalem would go out and dance in the vine-
yards. And what would they say? Young man, lift
up your eyes and see what you would choose for yourself. Do not fix your eyes on grace, but look to the
family, for (*Proverbs* xxxi, 30) *Favor is deceitful, and
beauty is vain: but a woman that feareth the Lord, she
shall be praised.*   (*Mishna*)

FROM CHAPTER IV

WOMEN

NASHIM

Childless Widows

(Tractate Yebamoth)

IF BRETHREN dwell together, and one of them die, and have no child, the wife of the dead shall not marry without, unto a stranger: her husband's brother shall go in unto her, and take her to him to wife (Deuteronomy xxv, 5).

And if the man like not to take his brother's wife, then let his brother's wife go up to the gate unto the Elders, and say: My husband's brother refuseth to raise up unto his brother a name in Israel; he will not perform the duty of my husband's brother.

Then the Elders of his city call him, and speak unto him; and if he stand to it, and say: I like not to take her. Then shall his brother's wife come unto him in the presence of the Elders and (perform the Halizah) loose his shoe from off his foot, and spit in his face, and shall answer and say: So shall it be done unto that man that will not build up his brother's house (Deuteronomy xxv, 7-8-9). [These words from the *Bible* make clear the basis of this tractate.]

A WOMAN whose husband went to a land beyond the sea, was advised that he had died. She remarried and subsequently her husband returned. She must leave one and the other, and must get a divorce from each one of them. She has no claim on either of them for her marriage settlement, her board, nor her clothes, and if she has taken anything from one and the other, she must return it to them. If a child was born to her by either of them, the child is a bastard. Neither of them will be defiled because of her, and neither one nor the other has any claim on whatever she finds, nor on her handiwork, nor can either of them set aside her vows. If she be the daughter of an Israelite, she is barred from marriage to a priest; if she be a daughter of a Levite, from eating of the tithe; and if a daughter of a priest, from eating of the Heave-offering. The heirs of neither of them may inherit her marriage settlement. If either of the husbands die, their brothers must perform the *Halizah*, but may not contract levirate marriage.

Rabbi Yosi says: Her dowry is a charge on her first husband's estate.

Rabbi Eleazar says: Her first husband has a right to whatever she may find, or to her handiwork, and may void her vows.

Rabbi Simon says: If the brother of her first husband cohabited with her, or performed the *Halizah*, her co-wife is exempt from levirate marriage, and a child begotten by her first husband is not a bastard. But if she were married again without the consent of court, she may return to her first husband. If she married again with the consent of the court, she must be divorced and she must make the sin offering. It is the authority of the court that makes her exempt from the sin offering. If the court permitted her to remarry but she went out and disgraced herself, she must bring a sin offering; because the court's permission was only to marry. (*Mishna*)

"AND must get a divorce from each one of them." It is quite obvious that she must get a divorce from the first husband. But why from the second, which is nothing else but a case of adultery?

Rabbi Huna answers: This is a precaution. It may be said that the first husband had divorced her, and the second had lawfully married her, and a married woman may leave her husband without a writ of divorce. If so, how is the latter clause to be explained, which says: If she was told: Thine spouse is dead, and she was betrothed, and her husband returned, she may return to him. One may say this time too that her first husband divorced her, and that the second married her, and that consequently a married woman may leave her husband without a writ of divorce. In reality she does not need a divorce. If so it may appear that the first husband had married his divorced wife after she was betrothed. This is in accordance with Rabbi Yosi ben Kipper who maintained that the remarrying of one's divorced wife after a marriage is forbidden, but after a betrothal is permissible.

"She has no claim on her marriage settlement." Why did the Rabbis provide a marriage settlement? The

Rabbis provided a marriage settlement so that it wouldn't be easy for a man to divorce his wife. But in this case let it be easy for him to divorce his wife.

(*Gemara*)

FROM CHAPTER X

THE ceremony of the *Halizah* must be performed before three judges, even if they be laymen. If the widow performed it with a shoe, it is valid; if with a sock, it is not valid; if with a heeled sandal, it is valid; but if it had no heel, it is not valid; if from below the knee, it is valid; if from above the knee, it is not valid. If she performed the *Halizah* with a shoe that did not belong to the man, or with a sabot, or with a left shoe that was worn on the right foot, it is valid. With a shoe that was too big, but he could walk in it, or with one that was too small but covered most of his foot, it is valid.   (*Mishna*)

SAID Raba, in the name of Rabbi Cahana, in the name of Rab: If the prophet Elijah should appear and say that *Halizah* may be performed with a shoe, he would be followed, but if he would say *Halizah* must not be performed with a sandal, he would not be followed, because it has long since been established by the people that *Halizah* is being performed with a sandal.

"Above the knee." Rabbi Cahana objects (*Deuteronomy* xxviii, 57) *And toward her young one that cometh out from between her feet.* Abaya answered: When a woman kneels to give birth she presses her heels against her thighs and thus gives birth. Come and hear: (2 *Samuel* xix, 24) *And had neither dressed his feet nor trimmed his beard.* This is a euphemistic phrase. Come and hear: (1 *Samuel* xxiv, 3) *And Saul went in to cover his feet.* This, too, is a euphemistic phrase. Come and hear: (*Judges* iii, 24) *Surely he covereth his feet in his summer chamber.* This is a euphemistic phrase: (*Judges* v, 27) *At her feet,* etc. This, too, is a euphemistic phrase.

Rabbi Yohanan said: Seven indulgencies in sexual intercourse had that wicked man, Sisera, the day he fled from Barak and Deborah. For it was said: (*Judges* v, 27) *At her feet he bowed, he fell, he lay down: at her feet he bowed, he fell: where he bowed, there he fell down dead.* But surely Jael had pleasure from that sin.

Rabbi Yohanan answered in the name of Rabbi Simon ben Yohai: Every good deed committed by an evil person is evil unto the righteous. As it is said: (*Genesis* xxxi, 24) *Take heed that thou speak not to Jacob either good or bad.* Obviously, when it is spoken of evil; but why of good deeds? Because the good deeds of the wicked are evil to the righteous. By all means, because he may mention to him the name of his idol. But what evil could it cause here? He may inoculate her with sensual lust. As Rabbi Yohanan said: When the serpent copulated with Eve, he inoculated her with lust. For the Israelites who stood at Mount Sinai, lust terminated, but the lust of those who did not stand at Mount Sinai was not terminated.   (*Gemara*)

FROM CHAPTER XII

The Marriage Contract

(TRACTATE KETHUBOTH)

A VIRGIN is to be married on the fourth day of the week, and a widow on the fifth day. Because the court is in session in the towns twice a week, on the second and on the fifth days of the week. So if a man questions the virginity of his newly wedded wife, he may bring suit in court the next morning.

The marriage settlement of a virgin is two hundred *zuz* and of a widow one hundred *zuz*. A virgin who becomes a widow after betrothal, or a divorcee or an *Haluzah,* her marriage settlement is two hundred *zuz,* and if her virginity is questioned, may be taken to court.

An adult who had intercourse with a minor, or a minor who had intercourse with an adult, or one whose hymen was broken by accident, her settlement is two hundred *zuz,* according to Rabbi Meir. The sages say: If it was due to an accident, her settlement is one hundred. A virgin who becomes a widow after betrothal, a divorcee or an *Haluzah,* her marriage settlement is one hundred *zuz,* and the question of her virginity cannot be taken to court. (*Mishna*)

157

SOMEONE came to Rabban Gamaliel and complained:
I have found an "open door". Said the Rabbi: You
might have moved it aside. I will give you an illustration: A man walked in the darkness of the night; he
came upon a door. If he happened to move it, he found
it open; if he did not happen to move it, it was locked.

Someone came to Rabban Gamaliel ben Rabbi and
said: Master, I have had intercourse with my newly
wedded wife and found no blood. The wife said: Master, I was a virgin. The Rabbi said: Bring me the sheet.
When the sheet was brought he took it and soaked it in
water and washed it, whereupon he found many drops
of blood in the water. Then the Rabbi said to the husband: Go home and be happy with thine lot.

Someone came to Rabban Gamaliel ben Rabbi and
said: Master, I have had intercourse with my newly
wedded wife, and found no blood. The wife said: Master, I am still a virgin. Said the Rabbi: Bring before
me two bondwomen, one a virgin and one that has been
with man. They brought him two bondwomen; one a
virgin, and one that had been with a man. He made
them sit on a keg of wine. The one who had been with
a man, the aroma of wine came through her, but the
virgin,—the aroma of the wine did not go through her.
He then made the wife sit on a keg of wine, and the
smell did not go through her. The Rabbi then said to
the husband: Go home and be happy with thine lot.

(Gemara)

IF THE woman lost her marriage contract, or hid it,
or it was burnt, and if she produce witnesses that any
one of the following took place: If they danced before

her, played before her, if the cup of glad tidings was passed before her, or the sheet of virginity was exhibited: if she can produce proof of any one of these things, her marriage dowry shall be two hundred *zuz*.   (*Baraitha*)

THE Rabbis taught: How does one dance before a bride? The House of Shamai says: According to what the bride is like. The House of Hillel argues: You say beautiful, charming bride. The House of Shamai argued with the House of Hillel: Suppose she is deformed or blind, how can one say "beautiful and charming bride"? The *Torah* has taught us: (*Exodus* xxiii, 7) *Keep thee far from a false matter*. The House of Hillel answered to the House of Shamai: As you wish. If one has brought back a bad bargain from the market, should one praise his purchase to his face or deride it? —No doubt one should praise it. Therefore the sages said: A person should always be pleasant to other people. Rabbi Dimi said: In the West they sing thus before a bride; No eye-paint, no rouge and no waving of hair, and still "charming and most beautiful".

When Rabbi Zera was ordained they sang before him: No eye-paint, no rouge and no waving of hair and still "charming and most beautiful".

When Rabbi Ammi and Rabbi Assi were ordained they sang before them as follows: Ordain unto us such as these, such as these, but do not ordain unto us scoundrels and idiots.

When Rabbi Abbahu came from the academy to the palace of the king, maidens of the court came forth before him and sang; Prince of his people, leader of his nation, brilliant light, blessed be thy coming in peace.

It is said of Rabbi Yehuda bar Elai that he used to take a twig and dance before the bride and say: Beautiful and charming bride. Rabbi Samuel ben Rabbi Isaac would also dance with twigs. Rabbi Zera said: That Graybeard is putting us to shame. When Rabbi Samuel passed away a pillar of fire came between him and the whole world. And it has been known that such a pillar of fire appears only once and at the most twice in a generation. Rabbi Zera said, it was on account of the twig. Others said it was because of his fine character, and some said because of his folly.

Rabbi Aha took the bride on his shoulder and danced. The Rabbis asked him: May we do the same? He answered: If the bride be on your shoulder like a beam, you may; otherwise not.

Rabbi Samuel ben Nahmani said in the name of Rabbi Jonathan: One may gaze upon the face of the bride all the seven days of the wedding festival, so as to make her husband more desirous of her. But the law is not in accord with this. (*Gemara*)

FROM CHAPTER I

THE seducer pays three kinds of compensations. The violator, four kinds. The seducer must pay for indignity and blemish, and the legal fine. The violator must add to it compensation for the pain that he caused. What is the difference between a violator and a seducer? The violator causes pain; the seducer does not cause pain. The violator pays the penalty at once; the seducer only if he declines the girl. The violator must drink out of his pot; but the seducer, if he wishes, may decline the girl.

How does the violator drink out of his pot? He is compelled to marry her even if she be deformed, blind; even if she be afflicted with boils. But if she was found to be immoral, and therefore not fit to marry an Israelite, he does not have to live with her. For it is said: (*Deuteronomy* xxii, 29) *and she shall be his wife.* This means a wife that is suitable for him.

What is the compensation for indignity? It is all in accordance with the case of the offender and the offended. And in case of blemish? The girl is considered as if she were a bondwoman that is put up for sale. How much was she worth before, and how much is she worth now?

The fine is the same for all, and whenever there is a sum fixed by the law, it remains the same for all.

(*Mishna*)
FROM CHAPTER III

THE father exercises authority over his daughter as regards her betrothal, through money, a contract, or intercourse. To him belong all that she may find and all her handiwork, and he may void her vows. He also receives her writ of divorce. But he may not use her property during her lifetime. If she gets married, her husband supersedes the father, because he has the right to her property during her lifetime; but the husband is responsible for her maintenance, her ransom, if she be captured, and for her burial. Rabbi Yehuda said: Even the poorest in Israel will provide not less than two flute players and one wailing woman.   (*Mishna*)
FROM CHAPTER IV

THE following are the chores which a woman must perform for her husband: Grind flour, bake, launder, cook, nurse her son, make ready his bed, and work at the wool. If she brought him one bondwoman she need not grind the flour, nor bake, nor launder. If she brought two, she need not cook, nor nurse her son. If she brought three, she need not make his bed, nor work at the wool. If she brought four she may sit in a chair all day long. Rabbi Eleazar said: Even if she brought him a hundred bondswomen, he should compel her to work at the wool, for idleness leads but to unchastity. Rabbi Simon ben Gamaliel said: If a man vowed not to permit his wife to work, he should be made to divorce her, and give her her marriage settlement, for idleness leads to ennui.

If a man vowed not to sleep with his wife, the House of Shamai says: She may agree to two weeks. The House of Hillel says: One week only. Students may go away to the colleges without their wives' permission for thirty days; laborers may stay away from their wives only one week. The *Torah* prescribed the marital duties as follows: Men who are unoccupied: every day; laborers, twice a week; ass-drivers, once a week; camel-drivers once in thirty days; sailors, once in three months. These are the words of Rabbi Eliezer.

If a woman does not consent to her husband, he may reduce her marriage allotment by seven *denars* each week. Rabbi Yehuda says: seven *tropaiks*. How long may he keep on reducing? Until her whole allotment is used up. Rabbi Yosi says: He may keep it up forever. If, perchance, an inheritance falls to her lot, he may put a claim upon it. If a man does not consent to his wife, her allotment is to be increased by seven *denars* each week. Rabbi Yehuda says: three *tropaiks*.

IF A man maintains his wife through a third person, he must allot to her not less than two measures of wheat or four measures of barley. He must also give her half a measure of beans and half a *loog* of oil, a measure of dried figs or a *minah* of pressed figs. If he cannot provide these he may substitute other fruits in their place. He must also provide her with a bed, and a mattress. If he has no mattress, a mat. He must also give her a cap for her head and a girdle for her loins and shoes at each of the festivals and clothing to the amount of fifty *zuz*, each year. If he cannot give her new clothes for the summer and old clothes for the rainy season, he must provide clothes to the value of fifty *zuz* in the rainy season, and she may clothe herself with worn garments in the summer. The used garments remain her property. He must also give her a silver coin for her needs. And she is to dine with him each Sabbath eve. If he does not give her the silver coin for her needs, her handiwork belongs to her. How much must she produce for her husband? In Judea she must weave for him the weight of five *selahs*; in Galillee ten *selahs,* but if she is nursing a child, they must reduce the amount of her work and increase her food allowance. This is spoken of the poor, but the rich must provide according to their standing.   ' (*Mishna*)

GRINDING of flour. How come you to say a thing like that? You can interpret it: supervise the grinding of flour, but if you will, you can say: grinding with a hand mill. The *Mishna* does not teach in accordance with the views of Rabbi Hiya, for Rabbi Hiya taught: A woman is only for beauty, or only for the sake of the children she will bear. Further Rabbi Hiya taught: A woman is only good for the finery she wears. And Rabbi Hiya also stated: Whosoever wishes his woman to look nice should dress her in linen garments. Whosoever wishes his daughters to have a clear complexion should feed her young chickens and give her milk to drink before she is about to attain her maturity.

OUR Rabbis taught: A child should be nursed twenty-four months. From then on, it is as if it sucked a detestable thing. These are the words of Rabbi Eliezer.

Rabbi Joshua said: The child may nurse even for four or five years, but if it stopped at twenty-four months and then started again, then it should be regarded as if it were sucking a detestable thing.

The Rabbis taught: If a woman agrees to nurse someone's child, she must not nurse her own child or a friend's child at the same time. If she agreed to a small fee, she still must eat plenty, and while she nurses, she must not eat anything that will be injurious to the milk.

A WOMAN that has her marital relations in a mill will have epileptic children; one that has intercourse on the ground will have children with long necks. A woman that steps on the blood of an ass will have scabby children. If she eats mustard, she will have hot tempered children. One who eats cress, will have bleary-eyed children. If she eats fish-soup, she will have children with blinking eyes. If she eats earth, she will have ugly children. One who partakes of intoxicating drinks will have dark children. The woman who eats meat and drinks wine will have strong children. If she eats eggs, her children will have big eyes. If she eats fish, her children will be very graceful. One who eats parsley will have beautiful children. One who eats coriander will have stout children. If she eats citrons, her children will have a pleasing scent. The mother of King Shapor's daughter ate citrons during her pregnancy, and the daughter used to be brought before her father as his finest perfume.

STUDENTS may go away to college, etc. For how long a period may they go with the permission of their wives?—For as long as they wish. What should be the usual time? Rab said: One month at college and one month at home. As it was said: (1 *Chronicles* xxvii, 1) *In any matter of the courses which came in and went out month by month throughout all the months of the year.*

Rabbi Yohanan said: One month at college and two months at home. As it was said: (1 *Kings* v, 14) *A month they were at Lebanon and two at home.*

For laborers, twice a week. Were we not taught, laborers once a week; how is this? Rabbi Hanina answered: There is no contradiction here. One speaks of those who work in the town where they live, while the other speaks of those who work away from their home town.

How often should the scholars perform their duties

to their wives? Says Rabbi Yehuda in the name of
Rabbi Samuel: Every Sabbath eve.

Yehuda the son of Rabbi Hiya and son-in-law of
Rabbi Yanai spent all his time at the academy but every
Sabbath eve he would go home. When he arrived one
could see a pillar of light before him. Once he was so
engrossed in his studies that he forgot to go home. When
Rabbi Yanai missed the sign he said: Cover his bed, because if Yehuda were alive, he surely would not fail to
do his duty towards his wife. This was (*Ecclesiastes*
x, 5) *as an error which proceedeth from the ruler,* for
Yehuda's soul went to its eternal rest.

Rabbi Hanania ben Hakinai went to the academy and
remained there twelve years. When he returned, the
streets in the town were changed and he could not find
his home. He sat himself down beside the river. There
he heard someone call: Daughter of Hakinai, daughter
of Rabbi Hakinai, fill thy pitcher with water and we will
go home. This maiden must belong to us, he thought,
and he followed her. When they came to the house, his
wife was sitting at the door and sifting flour. When she
raised her eyes and saw him, her heart stopped beating
and she passed away. Then the husband prayed to the
Lord: This poor soul, is that her reward? Have mercy
on her. And she came to life again.

Rabbi Akiba was a shepherd in the service of the
wealthy Ben Kalba Sabua, and Sabua's daughter saw
how noble and modest he was. She fell in love with him.
One day she addressed him. If I should get betrothed
to you, would you go away and devote your time to study
and become a scholar? Most surely, replied Akiba. They
were then secretly betrothed and she sent him forth to

the academy. When her father found out about it, he drove her out of his house and vowed that she would not receive any inheritance from him.

Rabbi Akiba spent twelve years at the academy; when he returned twelve thousand disciples followed him. While he was home he heard an old man say to his wife: How much longer do you choose to remain in living widowhood? However, she retorted: If he would listen to me, he would spend another twelve years in the academy.

Whereupon Rabbi Akiba said: It is, then, with her consent that I may go, and immediately departed to the academy for another twelve years. When he returned this time there were twenty-four thousand disciples who followed him.

When his wife was advised that he was on the way, she went forth to greet him. Her neighbor begged her to borrow some clothes and finery and attire herself in them. But she answered: (*Proverbs* xii, 10) *A righteous man regardeth the life of his beast.* When she approached him, she fell upon her face and kissed his feet. His servants wanted to drive her away, but Rabbi Akiba said: Leave her alone. All that is mine and all that is yours belongs to her.

When her father heard that a great man had come to town, he said: I shall go to him, he may release me from my vow. When he came, Rabbi Akiba asked him: Would you have made your vow if you knew that your daughter's husband was a great scholar? Sabua replied: If he but knew one chapter of the *Torah* or one article of law, I should never have made my vow. Whereupon Rabbi Akiba said: I am the man. Sabua fell upon his face and kissed his feet and then bestowed upon him half of his wealth.

The daughter of Rabbi Akiba did the same thing with Ben Azai. This is just as the people say: One sheep follows another, like the mother so is the daughter.

WHEN Rabbi Yehuda, the Prince, was about to die, he asked for his sons. When they appeared before him, he said to them: Be careful to respect your mother. The candles should remain lighted in their place. The table should always be set in its place, and the bed shall always be made up in its place. Joseph of Haifa and Simon of Ephrath who attended to me while I was alive, shall attend to me when I am gone.

Then he asked for the Sages of Israel. When the Sages of Israel arrived, he said to them: Do not mourn over me in the small towns. Reassemble the classes in the academy after thirty days. Simon, my son, is wise. My son, Gamaliel, is Prince, and Hanina ben Hama shall preside over the academy.

Then he asked for his son, Simon. When Simon came in, he instructed him in the orders of wisdom. Then he asked for his elder son, Gamaliel. When Rabbi Gamaliel came, he instructed him in the traditions and conduct of his office. He said to him: My son, conduct your principality with honor and cast bile among the disciples.

On the day that Rabbi Yehuda died, a voice appeared and announced: All those who were present at the death of the Rabbi will be destined for the world to come. A launderer who used to come to the Rabbi every day, did not appear that day. When he heard of the voice that appeared, he went up to the roof and jumped and was killed. The voice appeared again and announced: This launderer is also destined for the world to come.

The day before the Rabbi died, the Sages proclaimed a public fast and prayers for the life of the Rabbi. They further vowed that whoever would say the Rabbi died, would be killed.

The Rabbi's maid-servant went up to the roof and prayed: The angels want the Rabbi to join them and the mortals want the Rabbi to remain on the earth. May it please the Lord that the mortals be victorious over the angels. But when she saw how many times he had to go to the lavatory and how he suffered at the taking off and putting on of the phylacteries, each time, she prayed: May it please the Lord that the angels be victorious. But as the Rabbis did not stop their prayers for a moment, she took a crock and hurled it to the ground. The Rabbis stopped their prayers, and that moment the soul of Rabbi Yehuda departed.

The Rabbis told Bar Kapra to go in and investigate. When he went in, he found that the Rabbi was dead. He tore his garments and returned to the Rabbis and said: The angels and the mortals have gotten hold of the Holy Ark. The angels overpowered the mortals and the Holy Ark has been captured. Has his soul departed? they asked of him. You said it, he replied; I said nothing. *(Gemara)*

FROM CHAPTER V

Adultery

(Tractate Sotah)

IF A man be jealous of his wife, he may warn her, according to Rabbi Eliezer, before two witnesses. He may make her drink the bitter water on the evidence of two witnesses, or on his own evidence.

How does he warn her? If he says to her, before two witnesses: Don't talk to so-and-so. But if she spoke to the man, she is still allowed into the home and she may eat of the Heave-offering. If she secretly entered a house with him, and stayed there long enough to be defiled, she is barred from her home, and is barred from eating of the Heave-offering. If her husband should die she performs the rite of *Halizah,* but does not contract levirate marriage.

The *Sotah* used to be brought before the high court in Jerusalem and the judges addressed her in the same way as they addressed witnesses in capital cases. They would say to her: Our daughter, wine contributes much to sin; frivolity, much; childishness, much; evil neighbors, much. Behave yourself for the sake of the great

name that was written in holiness and which will not
be obliterated by water. And they say to her things
which neither she nor the family of her father's house
are worthy of hearing.

If she says: I have been defiled, she forfeits her marriage allotment and is sent away. If she says: I am
pure, she is brought to the Eastern gate which is near
the gate of Nicanor. There the suspected women drink
the bitter water. There the women are cleansed after
child birth, and there the lepers are cleansed. A priest
gets hold of her garments, if they get torn, they are
torn. If they are ripped, let them be ripped, so that her
bosom becomes uncovered. He undoes her hair. Rabbi
Yehuda says: If she has a beautiful bosom, he does not
uncover it. If she has beautiful hair, he does not undo
it. If she was dressed in white, he dresses her in black.
If she wore ornaments of gold chains and rings in her
nose and on her fingers, they are taken away from her
to make her look repulsive. Then the priest takes an
Egyptian rope and ties it above her breasts. Whoever
wants to gaze at her may come and gaze upon her, with
the exception of her slaves and bondswomen, because her
heart would be hardened by this. All the women are
permitted to gaze at her, as was said: (*Ezekiel* xiii, 48)
That all women may be taught not to do after lewdness.
(*Mishna*)
FROM CHAPTER I

THE Husband takes the meal offering out of the
Egyptian basket and puts it in the ministering vessel
and into her hand: the priest then puts his hands under
hers and waves it. After the waving he takes it to the

altar and lets a part of it go up in smoke, and the rest
is eaten by the priests. He then makes her drink the
bitter water and bring her sacrifice.   (*Mishna*)

FROM CHAPTER I

IF A man warned his wife and she secretly went out,
even if he heard of it from a flying bird he may give her
her marriage allotment and send her away. Thus says
Rabbi Eliezer. Rabbi Joshua, however, says: Not until
the women who spin yarn by the moonlight begin to talk
about it may he send her away.   (*Mishna*)

SAMUEL said: A man should rather marry a woman
of bad reputation than marry the daughter of a woman
who has a bad reputation. For the one comes from
pure stock, while the other comes from a tainted stock.
Rabbi Yohanan, however, said: A man should rather
marry the daughter of a woman of bad reputation,
but not the woman of bad reputation, because the one
is assumed to be chaste while the other one is not.
An objection. Does one marry a woman of bad reputation? The Rabbi answered: It should be interpreted:
If a man *had* married a woman of bad reputation. Rabbi
Tahlifa bar Maaraba learned from Rabbi Abahu: The
children of a loose woman are legitimate because the majority of the intercourses are ascribed to the husband.

Rab Amram asked. What is the case if she is a very
loose woman? If one maintains that a woman conceives
only shortly before her period, then no question may be
raised, because the husband does not know when this
occurs and cannot watch for her. However one that
maintains that a woman conceives after her cleansing,

can raise the question, because he knows when this takes place. Or cannot he tell anyway, since she is a very loose woman? The question remains without a solution.

(Gemara)

FROM CHAPTER VI

Divorces

(TRACTATE GITTIN)

ALL documents that have a Cuthean as a witness
are invalid, except writs of divorce and bills of emancipation. There was a case of a writ of divorce that was
brought before Rabban Gamaliel at Kfar Othnai. The
witnesses were Cutheans. He declared it valid. All
documents that are executed in the courts of the foreigners, though the witnesses be foreigners, are valid, except the writs of divorce and bills of slave emancipation.
Rabbi Simon says: These, too, are valid. They are not
to be honored only if they were executed by unauthorized
persons.   (*Mishna*)

FROM CHAPTER I

IF A man sent a writ of divorce to his wife and then
overtook the messenger or sent another messenger to
him and declared: The writ I gave to thee is void; it
becomes void.

Witnesses sign a document as a precaution, for the
general good.

If a man had pledged his slave as security and then set him free, the law declared that the slave is not liable for anything, but as a precaution the new master is compelled to give him a bill of emancipation, and the slave executes a bill of indebtedness for his value. Rabban Gamaliel says: He executes no document whatsoever. The one that set him free is liable. If a man is half slave and half free, he works one day for his master and one day for himself. This is according to the House of Hillel, but the House of Shamai said to them: This is well for the master, but not so for the man. He may not marry a slave, since he is half free, and he can not marry a free woman because he is half slave. Shall he remain unmarried forever? Was not the world made for fruition and increase? As was said: (*Isaiah* xlv, 18) *He created it not in vain, he formed it to be inhabited.* For the general good, the master is compelled to set the half slave free, and the man gives him a pledge for a half of his value. The House of Hillel changed their view and taught according to the decision of the House of Shamai.

If a man sold his slave to a foreigner or beyond the borders of the Land of Israel, the slave must be set free.

Captives should not be ransomed for more than their worth, to prevent abuses. For the same reason captives are not aided in their escape. Rabban Simon ben Gamaliel said: This is a precaution for the good of the captives. One does not buy scrolls of the *Torah,* phylacteries or *mezuzoth* for more than their value, to prevent abuses.

If a man sent away his wife because of her bad reputation, he may not take her back.

If a man sent away his wife because she is barren,
Rabbi Yehuda says: He may not take her back. But the
sages said: He may take her back.   (*Mishna*)

MANY procedures were laid down as a precaution
for the general good. A priest is called to read the
Torah first, then a Levite and then an Israelite, for the
sake of peace. A pit nearest the water-channel is filled
in first, for the sake of peace. The taking of animals
from their traps and fish from their nets is considered
somewhat like theft, for the sake of peace. Rabbi Yosi
says: This is outright theft.

The things found by a deaf-mute or an imbecile, or
a minor, are looked upon as belonging to them; and taking them away is somewhat like theft—for the sake of
peace. Rabbi Yosi says: This is outright theft. If a
poor man shakes the top of an olive tree, what is found
beneath it is considered like theft, for the sake of peace.
Rabbi Yosi says: Outright theft. One does not prevent
the poor of the foreigner from gathering gleanings, the
forgotten sheaf, and grain from the corner of fields, for
the sake of peace. A woman may lend to her neighbor
a sieve, a handmill, or an oven, though the neighbor is
suspected of transgressing the Sabbatical year, for the
sake of peace.

One may lend a hand in the field to a foreigner in
the Sabbatical year, but not to an Israelite.

One extends greetings to a foreigner, all for the sake
of peace.   (*Mishna*)

THREE kinds of writ of divorce are not valid, but, if
the woman remarried, the children are legitimate. If a
man wrote the writ in his own hand, but there are no
witnesses to it; there is no date on it, but there are witnesses; there is a date, but only one witness. Those are
the three kinds of writ of divorce that are not valid, but,
if the woman remarried, the children are legitimate.
Rabbi Eliezer says: Though there are no signatures of
witnesses on the writ, but it was given to the woman before two witnesses; it is valid, and she may collect her
marriage allotment from mortgaged property, because
the witnesses sign only as a precaution.

The House of Shamai says: A man must not divorce
his wife unless he has found her unfaithful. As was
said: (*Deuteronomy* xxiv, 1) *Because he hath found
some uncleanness in her.* The House of Hillel says:
He may divorce her if she only spoiled a dish for him because it was said: Uncleanness in anything. Rabbi
Akiba says: He may divorce her if he found another
that is more beautiful than his wife, because it was said:
(*Deut.* xxiv, 1) *If it come to pass that she find no favour
in his eyes.*   (*Mishna*)

WHEN Rab Papa was confronted with a Persian document that was made in a foreign court, he would call
in two foreigners, and without one knowing of the other,
let them read the document. If they both agreed as to its
contents, he would honor the document and, even, collect money on mortgaged property by such a document.

Rab Yehuda would take pains to read every document submitted to him. But Ula once said to him: You
need not go to this trouble, for Rabbi Eliezer, who was

the Head of the Land of Israel, had the documents read
to him, and then he signed them. Rabbi Nachman would
let the court scribes read the document to him, and then
he would sign.

Rabbi Shaman ben Aba said in the name of Rabbi
Yohanan: If a slave escapes from prison, he becomes
free, and furthermore his master is compelled to give
him a bill of emancipation. But Rab Simon ben Gamaliel taught that he returns to slavery. Rabbi bar Hanah
said in the name of Rabbi Yohanan that whenever Rab
Simon ben Gamaliel makes a statement in the *Mishna,*
the law is followed according to his decision. There is
the story of a woman slave of Mar Samuel that was
captured. She was ransomed and was returned to the
Rabbi with a message: We are of the opinion of Rabbi
Simon ben Gamaliel, but even if you follow the decision
of the Rabbis you may take her back, because we ransomed her as a slave. But as he had given up all hope
of ever recovering her, he would not take her back as a
slave, and she was not even required to get a bill of
emancipation.

Rabbi Zera said in the name of Rabbi Hanina, who
quoted Rabbi Ashi: The Rabbi said: When a slave marries a free woman in the presence of his master, he becomes free. Rabbi Yohana asked him: Do you know that
to be the ruling? I learned that according to Rabbi
Meir, if a man write a contract of betrothal for his female slave, she becomes betrothed, and the Sages said
that she is not betrothed. The explanation is like the
one of Rabbi ben Shila who ruled in an analogous case:
When the master puts the phylacteries on him. So is the

ruling, here. The slave becomes free, as the master
himself gives him the wife.

Rabbi Joshua ben Levi said: When a slave puts on
phylacteries in the presence of his master, he is free. If
the master borrows money from his slave, or appoints
him overseer of his estate, or if the slave puts on phylacteries or reads three passages from the *Torah,* in the
house of worship, in the presence of his master, does he
become free thereby? No, answered Rabbi ben Shila:
only when the master, himself, puts the phylacteries on
the slave.

When Rabbi Dime came he quoted Rabbi Yohanan
as saying: If a man said, just before he died, My female
slave so and so should be set free, his heirs are bound
to give her a bill of emancipation.

Rabbi Samuel ben Yehuda quoted Rabbi Yohanan: If
a man said at his death bed, my woman slave so and so
has been very kind to me, I want some kindness to be
done for her, the heirs are bound to do a deed of kindness for her. It is a duty to execute the will of the dead.

There was once a slave owned by two masters. One
set him free as to his half. The other bethought himself: If the Rabbis hear of it, they will compel me to set
him free. So he transferred him to his minor son. Rab
Joseph took this case to Rab Papa. He retorted: (*Oba-
diah* i, 15) *As thou hast done, it shall be done unto
thee: Thy reward shall return upon thine head.* We
all are aware that a child likes to play with coins. We
shall appoint a guardian for the child. He will jingle
some coins before him, and then the guardian will write
a bill of emancipation in the child's name.   (*Gemara*)

Betrothals

(Tractate Kiddushin)

A WIFE is acquired in three ways, and she can get her freedom in two ways. She is acquired through money, through a deed, or through sexual intimacy. And she can get her freedom by divorce, or through her husband's death. *(Mishna)*

THIS *Mishna* is in accord with Rabbi Simon, for Rabbi Simon taught: Why did the *Torah* say (*Deuteronomy* xxii, 13) *If a man take a wife,* and not if a woman is taken by a man? Because this is the way of the male to go out and look for the female, and it is not the custom for the female to look for the male. This is the same when someone loses an object. Who is looking for whom? The loser looks for the object, and not the object for the loser.

By money. How so? We have learned that the father exercises authority over his daughter in regard to her betrothal by money contract, or intercourse. How do we know that she can be acquired through money, and that the money belongs to her father? Rab Yehuda replied in the name of Rab: The scriptures say: (*Exodus* xxi, 11) *Then shall she go out free without money.* Her master does not receive any money, but money is given to another master, namely, the father. How about the money belonging to the girl? How is it that her father has authority over her betrothal? For it is written: (*Deuteronomy* xxii, 16) *I gave my daughter unto this man,* and she should get the money. Possibly this refers to a minor who has no right to accept her betrothal contract; but how about a grown girl, who has the right to accept her betrothal contract? She can betroth herself and take the money. It is written (*Numbers* xxx, 16) *In her youth in her father's house.* All gain of youth belongs to her father. The Rabbis taught: How is a wife acquired through money? If a man gave a woman money, or its equivalent, and said to her: Thou art betrothed to me; Thou art consecrated to me; Thou art a wife to me,—then she is betrothed to him. But if she gives the money to the man and says: I am betrothed to thee; I am consecrated to thee; I am a wife to thee,— she is not betrothed.   (*Gemara*)

A HEBREW slave is acquired by money or by a deed: and can free himself in the "seventh" year, or in the year of Jubilee or by paying for the outstanding time of his service. The Hebrew female slave has the advantage of being freed by signs of puberty. The slave who does not want to be freed in the "seventh" year is secured by having his ear bored, and is made free in the Jubilee or on his master's death.   (*Mishna*)

THE Rabbis taught: If the man stole a thousand, but he is worth five hundred, he is sold once and then sold again. If he stole five hundred, and he is worth a thousand, he is not sold at all. Rabbi Eliezer says: If his theft corresponds to his worth, he is sold, otherwise he is not sold at all. The Rabbis said: In the following arguments Rabbi Eliezer prevails over the Rabbis: If he stole five hundred but he is still worth a thousand, he is not sold; because the All Merciful said: (*Exodus* xxii, 3) *Then he shall be sold.* All of him, and not half of him and the All Merciful also said: (*Exodus* xxii, 3) *Sold for his theft;* not for half of his theft.

A slave is freed against her own will. Raba wanted to interpret this: against the master's will, but Abaya said to him: How is that? Does it mean that one gives the master a bond for the value?—Would that be right? A man has a pearl in his hand, and we will give him a potsherd for it? But Abaya explained: It is meant against the will of her father, because of the disgrace to the family. Then should the family of a Hebrew male slave be compelled to redeem him because of the disgrace to the family?—Then he may go and sell himself again. In the case of the female slave too, cannot the father go and sell her again? Were not we taught, however, she cannot be sold, and sold over again, and this is according to Rabbi Simon who taught: A man may sell his daughter for marriage, and sell her a second time. He may sell her over again. He may sell her in marriage after servitude, but not for servitude after marriage says Rabbi Simon. Just as you cannot sell a daughter for servitude after the marriage, one cannot sell her for servitude after servitude.   (*Gemara*)

A CANAANITE slave is acquired through money, through a bond or through the law of possession. He can redeem himself through money paid by others or through a bond of his own. This is according to Rabbi Meir. The sages, however, said: Through money of his own or by a bond of other people, providing the money belongs to other people.

Large cattle are acquired through delivery. Small cattle are acquired through lifting. This according to Rabbis Meir and Eliezer. The sages, however, said: Small cattle are acquired through pulling.

Secured property can be acquired by money, by a deed, or by the law of possession.   (*Mishna*)

THE Rabbis taught: Through possession in the following manner: If the slave loosened his shoe, if he carried his baggage for him to the bathing place, if he undressed him, bathed him, rubbed him, dressed him, put his shoes on, or if he lifted him, thus he acquired him. Rabbi Simon said: Possession is not greater than lifting; for by lifting, acquisition is valid everywhere. What does he mean? Rabbi Ashi explains: If the slave lifted the master he is thereby acquired by the master, but if the master lifted the slave, he did not acquire the slave. Rabbi Simon said: Possession should not be greater than lifting, since lifting is recognized everywhere as acquisition.

We are taught: A slave goes free because of the loss of an eye, a tooth, or a limb that grows not again. It is quite obvious that the slave goes free because of the loss of an eye or a tooth. This is stated in the *Torah*. But how do we apply this to other parts of the body? It is self-evident. An eye or a tooth are blemishes which grow not again, so the loss of other limbs that grow not again make the slave free.

THE Rabbis taught: The father has the following obligations towards his son: He must circumcise him, redeem him, teach him the *Torah,* take a wife unto him, and teach him a trade. Some say he must teach him to swim also. Rabbi Yehuda said: He that does not teach his son a trade, teaches him to rob. Teaches him to rob? How is that?—we may say: as though he taught him to rob.

The Rabbis taught: If one must study and is about to marry, he studies first and marries later. But if he cannot do without a wife, he marries first, and then he studies. Rab Yehuda said in the name of Samuel: The law is that he marries first and studies later. Said Rabbi Yohanan: What? with a stone around his neck he can study the law?

Rab Hisda praised Rab Hamnuna before Rab Huna. He called him a great man. Said Rab Huna to him: If he comes to you, bring him to me. When Rab Hamnuna came before Rab Huna, he saw that he had no shawl on him. He asked him: Why have you no shawl on you? Rab Hamnuna replied: Because I am unmarried. The Rabbi turned his face away from him and said: Take notice that you do not see me again until you are married. He was consistent with his principles. For he said: He who is twenty and is not married lives in sin. Does he really mean, lives in sin? You may say, in sinful thoughts.

Rabbi said, and the school of Rabbi Ishmael agreed

with him: Till the age of twenty, the Lord sits and waits.
When will the man take a wife unto himself? But
when he reaches twenty and had not taken a wife unto
himself, the Lord says: Let his bones be swollen.

Rab Hisda said: The reason I am more alert than
my colleagues is because I was married at sixteen. And
had I married at fourteen, I would have said to Satan,
an arrow in thine eye.

Rab said to Rabbi Nehemia ben Ammi: Marry him
off while you have your hand around your son's neck;
that is between sixteen and twenty. Others say: between
eighteen and twenty-four. The Rabbis taught: The evil
desire is very hard. Even his Creator called him evil.
It was said: (*Genesis* viii, 21) *For the imagination of
man's heart is evil from his youth.*

Rabbi Isaac said: The desire of man renews itself
every day and has designs on him. As it was written:
(*Genesis* vi, 5) *was only evil continually.* And Rabbi
Simon ben Levi said: The evil desire of man gets the
upper hand of him every day and wishes to destroy him.
As was said: (*Psalms* xxxvii, 32) *The wicked watcheth
the righteous, and seeketh to slay him.* And if the Lord,
blessed be He, would not prevail against him, as was
said: (*ibid.* 33) *The Lord will not leave him in his hand.*

The school of Rabbi Ishmael taught: If this repre-
hensible thing shall come upon thee, drag it into the
house of learning. If it be stone, it will melt. If it be
iron, it will fall to fragments. As it was said: (*Jeremiah* xxiii, 29) *Is not my word like as fire? saith the
Lord; and like a hammer that breaketh the rock into
pieces.* And if it is stone it will melt, as was said:
(*Isaiah* lv, 1) *Ho, everyone that thirsteth, come ye to*

the waters. And moreover it was said: (*Job* xiv, 19)
The waters wear the stones.

To take a wife to him. How do we know this? For
it was written: (*Jeremiah* xxix, 6) *Take ye wives and
beget sons and daughters; and take wives for your sons,
and give your daughters to husbands.* All this is said
of his sons, for they are in his hands. But what about
the daughters, are they in his hand too?—This is the
meaning. One gives her a dowry, clothing and adorn-
ments, so that man will desire her.

THE Rabbis taught: It was said: (*Exodus* xx, 12)
Honor thy father and thy mother. It is also said:
(*Proverbs* iii, 9) *Honor the Lord with thy substance.*
The Scriptures had compared, here, the honor of father
and mother with that of the Lord. It was said: (*Leviticus* xix, 3) *Ye shall fear every man his mother and his
father* and it was said: (*Deuteronomy* vi, 13) *Thou
shalt fear the Lord thy God and serve him.* The Scriptures thus compare the fear of the Lord to that of the
father and mother. It was said: (*Leviticus* xxiv, 15)
Whosoever curseth his God shall bear his sin. Thus the
Scriptures compare the blessings of father and mother
to the blessing of the Lord.

Said Rab Yehuda in the name of Samuel: Rabbi
Eliezer was once asked: How far should the honor of
father and mother extend? He answered: Go and see
how a non-Jew, Dama ben Nethinah of Ashkelon, be-
haved towards his father:

Once the sages wanted to buy from him precious
stones for the priest's breastplate. It would have brought
him a profit of 60,000 *denars,* and Rabbi Kahana thinks

it was 80,000. But the key to the jewel case was under the pillow of Dama's father and Dama would not wake him. The Lord rewarded him for it, for next year a red calf was born in his herd. When the sages of Israel came to him again, he said to them I know that if I demand it, you would give me all the money in the world for the red calf, which you need for your rites. But all I will ask of you is the amount I lost, because of the honor I paid to my father. Rabbi Hanina commented: If he who is not commanded, gets such a reward, how much more will be rewarded the man who was given a commandment and fulfills his commandment.

When Rabbi Dimi came he related: Once Dama sat, among Romans, wearing a gold-embroidered silken gown. His mother came in and tore the garment off, struck him on the head, and spat in his face. He, however, did not shame her.

Abimi, the son of Rabbi Abahu taught: One gives his father pheasants to eat, yet this drives him out of this world, because of the manner in which he gives it to him, while another makes his father work at the grindstone in the mill, and yet this will give him life in the world to come, for he does so with due honor to his parent.

Rabbi Abahu said: Here is an illustration, how my son Abimi fulfilled the commandment of honor to his father. Abimi had five ordained sons during the life of his father, but when Rabbi Abahu came knocking at the door, he himself would run to open it for him, shouting all the while: I am coming, I am coming, until he reached it.

One day his father said: Get me a drink of water.

While he was getting the water the father fell asleep.
Abimi bent over him and stood there till he awoke. He
was rewarded for it, for he succeeded in interpreting
the Song of Asaph, in the *Psalms*.

The Rabbis taught: What is fear and what is honor?
Fear means that the son does not stand in his father's
place, does not sit in his father's place, he does not contradict him and does not overrule him. Honor means
that he feeds him, clothes him, covers him, and leads him
in and out.

HE THAT is versed in the *Scripture*, the *Mishna* and
the way of the world will not sin easily, for it was said:
(*Ecclesiastes* iv, 12) *And a three-fold cord is not
quickly broken*. But he who is not versed in the *Scripture*, nor in the *Mishna*, nor in the ways of life, has no
place in the world.   (*Mishna*)

SAID Rabbi Eleazar in the name of Rabbi Zadok:
The righteous in this world are compared to a tree that
stands in a clean place, but whose branches spread over
an unclean place. If the branches are pruned off, the
tree is now entirely in a clean place. The Holy One
blessed be His name, brings suffering upon the righteous
in this world, so that they may inherit the world to come,
as was said: (*Job* viii, 7) *Though thy beginning was
small, yet thy latter end should greatly increase*. To
what are the evil compared? To a tree that stands in
an unclean place, but its branches spread to a clean place.
If the branches are pruned off, the tree remains entirely
in an unclean place. So does the Holy One, blessed be
His name, bestow goodness upon the sinners in this world,
but He shall destroy them and shall make them inherit

the lowest depths of perdition, as was said: (*Prov.* xiv,
12) *There is a way that seemeth right unto a man; but
the ends thereof are the ways of death.*

Once Rabbi Tarpon and the elders were in an upper
story in the house of Nitzza in Lydia. The question was
propounded: What is greater, study or action? Rabbi
Tarpon said: Action. Rabbi Akiba said: Study is greater.
Then all the rabbis agreed and said study is greater,
for study leads to action.

The Rabbis taught: He who eats in the street is like
a dog, and some say he is disqualified from being a witness.

Bar Kappara preached. The hot tempered gains
nothing but the effects of his hot temper. But the good
man partakes of the fruit of his good deeds. From a
man that knows no *Scripture,* no *Mishna,* and no ways
of life, one may have no benefit. For it was said:
(*Psalms* i, 1) *His seat is the seat of the scornful.*

(*Gemara*)
FROM CHAPTER I

A MAN may betroth himself personally or through
an agent. A woman may betroth herself personally or
through an agent. A man may betroth his grown daughter personally or through an agent.

If a man said to a woman: Be betrothed to me with
this date, or be betrothed to me with this, and one of
them is worth a *perutha,* the betrothal is valid; if not,
it is not valid. If he said: Be betrothed to me with this,
this and this, and they were together worth a *perutha,*
the betrothal is valid; if they are not worth a *perutha,*
it is not valid. If he said: Be betrothed to me with

this cup of wine, and it was found to contain honey, or
if he said: With this cup of honey and it was found to
contain wine, or with this silver *denar,* and it was found
to be of gold; or with this gold *denar* and it was found
to be of silver; if he said: Be betrothed to me with the
understanding that I am rich, and it was found that he
was poor, or if he said poor and he was found to be
rich; the betrothal is not valid.

Rabbi Simon says: If the advantage is on her side,
she is betrothed.

If he said to the woman be betrothed to me, because
I am a priest and he was found to be a levite. . . . If he
said because I have a grown daughter or a bondwoman
and he does not have them, or he said I have them not,
and he has them, or if he said that he had children and
he did not have them, or if he said he did not have children and had them. In all of these cases, though she may
say: It was in my heart to be betrothed to him, the betrothal is not valid, and this also holds good if she de-
ceived the man.   (*Mishna*)

IF HE can betroth himself through an agent is it not
self-evident that he can do it personally? Rabbi Joseph
said: Personally is preferable to doing it through an
agent. It is even said that herewith is injected a prohibition. This is in accordance with Rab Yehuda, who
quoted Rab: One is prohibited to be betrothed to a
woman before he has seen her, for upon seeing her he
may find something repugnant in her and she may be
detestable to him, and the All Merciful taught: (*Leviticus* xix, 18) *But thou shalt love thy neighbor as thyself.*
And this according to Rab Joseph applies to the woman,

too. But Resh Lakish disagrees. He says: There is no prohibition as regards the woman, for it is better to suffer in marriage than to live in widowhood.

"A man may betroth his grown daughter." He may betroth her when she is grown, but not when she is a minor. This agrees with Rab. For Rab Yehuda said in the name of Rab, some may say it was Rabbi Eleazar: It is prohibited to betroth a daughter while she is a minor, only when she is grown and declares: "I want so-and-so."

RAB Nahman said in the name of Samuel: When orphans come to divide the estate of their father, the court appoints a guardian for them, and he selects a proper portion for each of them. But when they become of age they can protest it. Rab Nahman, however, decided that they cannot protest, because what would become of the authority of the court? If then Rab Nahman decides thus against the court, what becomes of the authority of the court in this instance? But it is taught: If the valuation of the judges was one-sixth too high or one-sixth too low the sale is void. Rabbi Simon ben Gamaliel said: It is not void, otherwise where does the authority of the court come in? Said Rab Huna in the name of Rabbi Hinena: Rab Nahman ruled that the law is in agreement with the sages. There is no contradiction here. It is one thing when the judges made a mistake, and another thing when there was no mistake.

TEN measures of wisdom descended upon the world. Nine were taken by the Land of Israel and one was taken by the rest of the world. Ten measures of beauty descended upon the world. Nine were taken by Jerusalem and one by the rest of the world. Ten measures of wealth descended upon the world, nine were taken by Rome and one by the rest of the world. Ten measures of poverty descended upon the world. Nine were taken by Babylon and one by the rest of the world. Ten measures of rudeness descended upon the world. Nine were taken by Elam and one by the rest of the world. Was not rudeness supposed to descend to Babylon? For it was written: (*Zech.* v, 9) *Then lifted I up mine eyes, and looked, and behold, there came out two women, and the wind was in their wings; for they had wings like the wings of a stork; and they lifted up the ephah between the earth and the heaven. Then said I to the angel that talked with me, Whither do these bear the ephah? And he said unto me, to build it a house in the land of Shinar* (Babylon). Rabbi Yohanan says: This refers to hypocrisy and haughtiness, which descended upon Babylon. It came first to Babylon, but went then to Elam. But this is, indeed, not so, said the Master. What is the sign of rudeness but poverty, and poverty is to be found in Babylon. What is meant by poverty is poverty of learning, as it is written: (*Song of Solomon* viii, 8) *We have a little sister and she hath no breasts.* Rabbi Yohanan said: This refers to Elam, which had the advantages of learning, but not that of teaching. Ten measures of strength descended upon the world. Nine were taken by the Persians, and one by the rest of the world. Ten measures of vermin descended upon the world. Nine were taken by Medea, and one. . . . Ten measures of witchcraft descended upon the world. Nine were taken by Egypt, and one. . . . Ten measures of

plagues descended upon the world. Nine were taken
by the pigs, and one. . . . Ten measures of whoring descended upon the world. Nine were taken by Arabia,
and one. . . . Ten measures of impudence descended upon
the world. Nine were taken by Meshan, and one. . . .
Ten measures of gossip descended upon the world. Nine
were taken by woman, and one. . . . Ten measures of
blackness descended upon the world. Nine were taken
by the Ethiopians, and one. . . . Ten measures of sleep
descended upon the world. Nine were taken by slaves
and one by the rest of the world.   (*Gemara*)

IF A man betrothed a woman with the stipulation that
she has no vows and it was found that she had vows,
she is not betrothed. If she was betrothed without any
stipulations, and it was found that she had vows, she
may be sent away without her marriage allotment. If
she was betrothed with the stipulation that there are no
defects in her, and it was found that she possesses defects, she is not betrothed. If she was betrothed without
any stipulations, and if she was found to possess defects,
she may be sent away without her marriage allotment.
All defects which disqualify priests disqualify women.

If a man betrothed two women with what was worth
a *perutha* or one woman with what was worth less than a
perutha, even if he sends gifts to her later, the betrothal
is not valid, for the reason he sends his gifts is that they
have already been betrothed. This applies, also, to a
minor.

If a man betroths a woman and her daughter, or a
woman and her sister both at the same time, they are
not betrothed.

There was once the case of five women, among whom
were two sisters. A man lifted a basket of figs that
belonged to them—it contained the produce of the 7th
year—and said: With this basket you all are betrothed
to me, and one of the women accepted the basket on behalf of them all. The sages ruled that the sisters were
not betrothed. ,   (*Mishna*)

FROM CHAPTER II

IF A man betrothed a woman, and later says: I believed that she was the daughter of a priest, and she
proves to be the daughter of a levite. Or the daughter
of a levite, and she is the daughter of a priest. Or rich,
and she is poor, or poor, and she is rich. She is betrothed to him, for she did not deceive him. If a man
says to a woman: Be thou betrothed to me after I become a proselyte, or after thou becomest a proselyte, or
after I become free, or thou becomest free, or after
thine husband shall die, or after thine sister shall die,
or after thou shalt have performed the *Halizah* to thine
brother-in-law: she is not betrothed. This applies also
to one who said: If thine wife shall bear thee a female
child, it is betrothed to me. The child is not betrothed.
If a man said: Be betrothed to me on the condition
that I intercede for thee with the government or on condition that I work for thee as a laborer; if he interceded
on her behalf with the government or worked for her as
a laborer, she is betrothed. But if he did not, she is not
betrothed. If he said: Be thou betrothed to me on condition that my father consents. If the father consent,
she is betrothed, if not, she is not betrothed. If the
father die in the meantime, she is betrothed. But if the

son died, the father is instructed to say that he does not consent.

If a man says: I betrothed my daughter to some-one, but I do not know whom, and someone appears and says: I betrothed her, he is believed. If two appear and each says that he betrothed her, both are compelled to give her a writ of divorce, but if they are willing, one gives her a writ of divorce and the other marries her.

(*Mishna*)

RAB says: He is believed when it's a question of a divorce as no one will sin without any gain; but not believed as to marriage.

His passion may have persuaded him to say it. Rab Ashi says: He is believed to marry her. But Rab Ashi stipulates, however, if the woman says: I have been betrothed, and know not to whom I have been betrothed, and one appears and says: I betrothed her, he is not believed to marry her.

We were taught according to Rabbi Ashi: I betrothed my daughter and know not to whom. If one comes and says: I betrothed her, he is believed to marry her. If he married her and another came and says: I betrothed her, he is not believed and she is not forbidden to the husband. But if a woman says: I was betrothed and know not to whom, and one appears and says: I betrothed her, he is not believed, because the woman will shield the man.

RAB Yehuda said: If one had betrothed this woman before one witness, the betrothal is disregarded. Rab Yehuda was asked: Suppose both admit it? He was uncertain, yes or no.

A question was asked: If one witness charges that one's wife committed adultery? Abaya says: The witness is believed. Rabbi says: This is a case of incest, and in a case of incest two witnesses are needed. Abaya said the following case proves it to me: Mar-Samuel had a blind man who used to recite the law for him every day. One day the man did not appear, so the Rabbi sent a messenger for him. While the messenger took one road, the blind man entered, coming through a different road. When the messenger returned, he announced that the blind man's wife committed adultery. Mar-Samuel said to the blind man, if you believe him send your wife away; but if you don't believe him, don't send her away. If you believe him means that the witness is not a robber. And Rab said: If you believe him as if it were two witnesses, send her away, otherwise don't send her away.

Abaya said: I also learn this from the following story:

Once King Yanai went to Kohalith in the wilderness and conquered sixty cities. When he returned he was very happy. He invited all the sages of Israel and said to them. Our forefathers ate mallow when they were building the Temple. Let us, too, eat mallow, in remembrance of our forefathers. So mallow was served on golden tables and they ate. Among them there was one Eleazar ben Poyra, a scoffer and an evil-minded man, and he said to King Yanai: "O King Yanai! The heart of the Pharisees is against thee." What shall I do? asked the King. Test them by the gold plate between thine eyes. So he tested them with the gold plate between his eyes. There was an old man there by the name of Yehuda ben Gedidiah. And Yehuda ben Gedidiah said to the King, "Oh King Yanai, the crown of royalty is enough for thee. Leave the crown of priesthood to the descendants of Aaron." Now there was talk that Yanai's mother was once a captive in Modin (This would make Yanai ineligible for priesthood), but this charge was investigated, and was never substantiated. The Sages of Israel departed in anger. Whereupon Eleazar ben Poyra said to King Yanai: "This is the law, even for the meanest in Israel, and thou art a King and High Priest. Art thou bound by the same law? Then what shall I do?" "If thou wilt listen to my advice, trample them down." "Then what shall become of the *Torah?*" "The *Torah* is rolled up, lying in the corner, whoever wants let him come and study." Said Rabbi Nahmai ben Israel: Immediately heresy entered into his soul, for he should have answered this applies to the written law, but how about the oral law? And this evil was spread through Eleazar ben Poyra. All the Sages of Israel were slain. And the world became desolate till Simon ben Shetah appeared and restored the *Torah* to its former position.

Now how does the case stand? Shall we say that there were two witnesses who said that she was a captive, and two that said she was not? Shall we believe one or the other? Therefore it must have been one witness who testified that she was a captive, and two who testified that she was not. Otherwise we would say that one would be believed. (*Gemara*)

RABBI Tarfon says: Bastards can be made pure. In what manner? A bastard marries a slave, the offspring is born a slave, but if he is later emancipated he becomes a free man. Rabbi Eliezer says: That is but a bastard slave. (*Mishna*)

A QUESTION. Does Rabbi Tarfon mean that this is at the very outset, or that it is already done? Come and hear. Rabbi Tarfon was asked: You have purified the male, but you have not purified the female. Now if you mean at the very outset, then let a female bastard go and marry a slave? A slave has no paternity. Come and hear: Once Rabbi Simlai said to his host, who was a bastard: Had I known you before, I could have made your sons to be pure. Surely! if you say that it is at the very outset; but if you say only if it has already been done, then what could he advise him? He would have told him to steal something and be sold as a Hebrew slave. From this you conclude that Rabbi Tarfon means at the very outset. Rabbi Yehuda said in the name of Samuel: The law is in accordance with Rabbi Tarfon. (*Gemara*)

FROM CHAPTER III

IF A man says: This son of mine is a bastard, he is not believed. Even when both parents say that the child in the mother's womb is a bastard, they are not believed. Rabbi Yehuda says: They are believed. (*Mishna*)

WHY say both parents? It is quite obvious that the father, who cannot be certain of the parentage, is not believed, but the mother who is sure of the parentage, why, too, is she not believed? It is self-evident that they

should not be believed when the child enjoys the presumption of being spotless, but in the case of a child who
is still in the womb and does not enjoy the presumption
of spotlessness, they are still not believed.

Rabbi Yehuda says: They are believed. We are
taught: (*Deuteronomy* xxi, 17) *He shall acknowledge
him before the others.* It follows: A man is believed
when he says: This son of mine is my first born. He
is also believed when he says: This one is the son of a
divorcee, this one is the son of a *Haluzah*. But the Sages
ruled that he is not believed.   (*Gemara*)

A MAN must not stay alone with two women. But
one woman may stay alone with two men. Rabbi Simon
says: One man may stay with two women if his wife is
with him, and he may sleep with them in an inn, because
his wife keeps watch over him. A man may stay alone
with his mother and with his daughter, and he may sleep
with them in the same bed. But if they become of age
she must sleep in her clothes, and he in his clothes.

(*Mishna*)

"BUT one woman." Rabbi Yehuda said in the name
of Rab: This is spoken only of respectable men and
women. Even ten men must not stay alone with a
loose woman. There was a case once when ten men
carried a woman out on a bier. Rabbi Joseph said: We
have proven that ten men will get together to steal a
beam, and will not be ashamed of each other.

Here is another proof: Two scholars are sent with
the man so that he won't have intercourse with the
woman on the way. Scholars, but not ordinary people.
Only scholars, because they know and can warn him.

Rab and Rab Yehuda were once walking on the road. There was a woman walking in front of them. Said Rab to Rab Yehuda: "Run faster away with perdition." "But you yourself said that it was all right with respectable people." "Who says that respectable people means men like you and me?" "Who then?" "Such as Rabbi Hanina and Rabbi Papi and their colleagues."

Rabbi Meir would scoff at transgression. One day Satan appeared to him on the other side of the river, disguised as a woman. As there was no bridge across, he grabbed a rope and began to tow himself across. When he reached the middle of the river, Satan let go, and said: Had they not proclaimed in Heaven: Take heed of Rabbi Meir and his learning, I would have valued your blood at two *mahs.*

Rabbi Akiba used to scoff at transgression. One day Satan appeared to him, disguised as a woman, on the top of a palm. Akiba grasped the palm and began to ascend. When he reached the middle, Satan let him go and said: Had they not proclaimed in Heaven: Take heed of Rabbi Akiba and his learning, I would have valued your blood at two *mahs.*

Pelimo used to say each day: A bolt in thine eye, Satan. One Eve of Atonement Satan appeared before him disguised as a beggar and knocked on his door. Bread was brought out to him. Whereupon Satan said: On a day like this everyone is within, shall I be outside? So he was asked to come in and they gave him bread. Whereupon he said: On a day like this everyone sits at the table, shall I sit alone? So he was asked to sit at the table. His body was all covered with sores and he conducted himself repulsively. Pelimo said to him: Sit

properly. Then Satan asked for a goblet. He was given
the goblet and he began to cough in it and spat his phlegm
into it. He was scolded. Whereupon he fell and died.
Whereupon a voice cried: "Pelimo killed a man, Pelimo
killed a man." So he ran and hid in a privy. Satan followed him. When he saw how Pelimo was suffering he
let himself be recognized and said: "Why do you talk
that way every day?" "What should I say?" inquired
Pelimo. "You should say: The All-Merciful upbraid
Satan."

Rab Hiya ben Ashi used to fall upon his face and
pray: All-Merciful, protect us from evil desire. When
one day his wife heard him, she reflected: It is so many
years that he kept away from me, why does he pray in
this manner? One day when he was studying in his
garden, she dressed herself up and paced before him,
back and forth several times. Whereupon he asked her:
"Who are you?" "I am Hirtha, the courtesan", she
answered, "and have returned only today." And when
he desired her, she said to him: "Get me that pomegranate from the top of the tree." He went up and got it
for her. When he returned home, his wife was just making the fire in the oven. So he went up and sat in it.
She said to him: "What does this mean?" He answered
her: "So and so happened to me." Whereupon she replied: "It was I", but he would not believe her until she
gave him proof thereof. "Nonetheless", he said, "my
intentions were sinful."   (*Gemara*)

A BACHELOR must not teach children, and a woman
must not teach children. Rabbi Eleazar says: Also
one who has no wife must not teach children. Rabbi

Yehuda says: A bachelor must not tend cattle, nor may two bachelors sleep under one cover. But the Sages permit it. One whose business is with women must not stay alone with women. And a man should not teach his son a woman's craft. Rabbi Meir says a man should teach his son a clean and easy trade, and let him look up to those that possess riches and wealth, for there is no trade that there are riches and poverty in it, and riches do not come from trade, nor does poverty, for all depends on merit.

Rabbi Simon ben Eleazer says: Have you ever seen a wild beast or bird that has a trade? And yet they sustain themselves without much trouble, and they were created to serve me, while I was created to serve my Maker. Is it not right that I shall sustain myself without trouble? But I have turned to evil and so despoiled my livelihood.

Abba Gurian of Zaidan says in the name of Abba Guria: A man should not teach his son to be: an ass-driver, or a camel-driver, or a barber, or a sailor, or a shepherd, or a shopkeeper, for all these trades are trades of thieves. Rabbi Yehuda said on his own account: The ass-drivers are mostly evil, but the camel-drivers are mostly honest. The sailors, most of them, are pious. The best of the medicine men may go to Hell, and the most honest of the butchers is a partner of Amalek. Rabbi Nehorai says: I keep away from all the trades in the world, and teach to my son the *Torah* only. Because a man gets his rewards in this world and the principal is secured for him for the world to come. But all other professions are not like that. For when a man gets sick or becomes old or is suffering and cannot engage in his work, he dies from starvation. But the *Torah* is not like that. For it guards him from all evil, and gives him a future and hope in his old age.

The Rabbis taught: He whose business is with women has a sullen disposition, as for instance: The goldsmiths, carders, a mill cleaner, a hawker, a peddler, weavers, barbers, launderers, blood-letters, bath attendants and tanners. They may not be crowned King or High Priest. Why? Not because they are unfitted, but because of their mean occupation.

Bar Kappra discoursed: Always teach your son an easy and clean trade. What is it? Rabbi Yehuda replied: "Needlepoint embroidery!"

It was taught: There is no trade that will disappear from the world. Happy is he who sees his parents in a superior trade, and woe to him who sees his parents in a mean trade. The world cannot do without a perfume maker and without a tanner. Happy is he whose trade is perfume making, and woe to him who is a tanner. The world cannot exist without male and female. Happy is he whose children are male and woe to him whose children are female.   (*Mishna*)

FROM CHAPTER IV

LAW

NEZIKIN

Civil Law

(Tractate Baba Kamma)

THERE are four primary causes of damage: The ox, the pit, the despoiler and fire. The ox is not like the despoiler, and the despoiler is not like the ox. Nor is either of these two, in which there is life, as the fire in which there is no life; nor are these whose way is to go forth and create damage, as the pit, whose way is not to go forth and create damage. The only thing that they have in common is that they cause damage, and that it is the owner's duty to watch out for them and prevent their causing any damage. And if any of them has caused any damage, the man responsible for them must pay for it with the best of his estate. (*Mishna*)

WHEN we speak of primary causes, then there must also be secondary causes. Are these other classes of damage equal to the first or not? ...

Rab Papa said: Some of the subdivisions are equal to the primary causes while others are not.

The Rabbis taught: There are three primary classes

of damage with regard to the ox. The Horn, the Tooth, and the Hoof. Whence do we know of the Horn? The Rabbis taught: (*Exodus* xxi, 28) *If it will gore.* There is no goring, but with a horn, as it was said: (1 *Kings* xxii, 11) *And Zedekaiah the son of Chenaaiah made him horns of iron: and he said, thus saith the Lord, With these shalt thou gore the Syrians,* and it is further said: (*Deut.* xxxiii, 17) *His glory is like the firstling of his bullock, and his horns are like the horns of unicorns: With them he shall gore the people,* etc.

For what purposes is the "further" quotation?—Because one may argue that the teaching of the Pentateuch cannot be deduced from the Prophets. Therefore it is stated: *His glory is like,* etc. But is this then a deduction? Is it not rather only an indication that by "goring" we are to understand that it means goring with a horn?—Indeed one could believe that the Almighty made the distinction between the harmless and the dangerous only as regards the severed horn, while if the horn is still attached to the animal it is always regarded as dangerous. Therefore it is said: *His glory is like the firstling of his bullock,* etc.

What are the subdivisions of Horn?—Collision, Biting, Falling and Kicking. Goring is surely considered a primary cause of damage, for it is written: (*Exodus* xxi, 35) *If it will gore.* Why should this not also apply to Collision, for it is written: (*Ibid.*) *If it will collide*—Here by collision we understand also goring. Indeed we were taught the passage begins with "collision" and ends with "goring"; this is to enlighten us that goring and colliding mean the same thing. Why is the word goring used with regard to humans, while with regard to animals we use the term colliding?—Man who has the faculty of judgment is, as a rule, injured through goring, but an animal, which possesses no such faculty, is, as a rule, injured through collision. . . .

What are the divisions of Pit? . . . It may refer to a stone, or a knife, or baggage that one left on a public thoroughfare, which has caused injury to someone. According to Samuel and Rab, if they were abandoned they would be in the same class as Pit, but if they were not abandoned, then, according to Samuel, who maintains that all such damages are included in the class of Pit, they would be classed as Pit, while according to Rab, who maintains that all such damages should be judged according to the rules which apply to the Ox, these would be put in the same class as the Ox.   (*Gemara*)

FIVE are considered harmless, while five are considered dangerous. Cattle are not considered dangerous whether to gore, to push, to bite, to fall down, or to kick. The tooth of an animal is considered as a danger, for an animal will consume everything that is fit for it to eat; a leg is considered as a danger, for it will break or trample as it goes along; and so is an ox that has become unmanageable, an ox that causes damage to private property; and likewise a human being. The wolf, the lion, the bear, the leopard, and the serpent are all considered as a danger. Rabbi Eliezer says: if they have been tamed, they are not considered a danger, but the serpent is always considered a danger. What is the difference between the harmless and the dangerous? The harmless pays half damages of its own body while the dangerous pays full damages out of the best of the estate.   (Mishna)

THE tooth of an animal is considered a danger in that it consumes everything that is fit to eat. A beast is considered a danger in so far as it will consume fruit and vegetables; but if it has consumed clothing or utensils, the owner pays only half damages. This applies only if the damage was done on the private property of the injured, but if it was caused in a public place, the owner is exempt from payment. If the beast derived a benefit from what it consumed, the owner pays to the extent of the benefit that the animal derived from it. In what instance does the owner pay for the benefit that the animal derived from it? If the animal consumed some food from the stalls in the midst of the market, the owner pays to the extent of the benefit that the animal derived from it; but if it consumed something from the back alleys of the market; he pays to the extent of the damage that it caused. If it consumed food from the entrance of a shop, he pays only to the extent of the benefit, but if from the inside of the shop, he must pay for the full damage that it caused.   (*Mishna*)

THE Rabbis taught: The tooth is considered a danger in that it consumes everything that is fit to eat. How? If a beast enters the property of the injured, and eats food that was fit for it, and drinks liquids that were fit for it; the owner pays full damages. And this applies, also, to an animal that has entered the property of the injured and torn an animal to pieces and eaten its flesh;

the owner pays full damages. This applies, also, to a cow that has consumed barley, or an ass that has consumed beans, or a dog that has licked up some oil, or a pig that has devoured a piece of meat; for these, the owner pays full damages. Rab Papa said: Now also we say that foods which ordinarily are not considered food fit for the particular animal, but which under pressing circumstances they consume, must be considered fit food for the animal. In case a cat has eaten dates, or an ass has eaten fish, the owner must pay full damages.

It happened once that an ass consumed some bread and ruined the basket. Rab Yehuda ordered payment of full damages for the bread, but only half damages for the basket.—Why so? If it is usual for the ass to eat bread, is it not also usual for it to ruin the basket? First it consumed the bread, and then it ruined the basket. But can we say that bread is the usual food of an ass? I shall point out a contradiction. If an animal has consumed bread, meat, or a cooked dish, the payment is only for half damages. Does this apply to a domestic animal? —No, this applies to a wild animal. To a wild animal? Does not a wild animal usually eat meat?—No, the meat was roasted. But if you wish, I can say that this refers to a deer. If you wish, I can also say that it refers to a domestic animal when it has consumed the bread that was lying on a table.

A goat saw some turnips on top of a barrel. It climbed up and ate the turnips, and in doing so broke the barrel. Rab ordered full damages to be paid for the turnips and for the barrel. He explained that as it was usual for a goat to eat turnips, it was also usual for it to climb up for them.

RAB Hisda said to Rami ben Hama: Why weren't
you at the academy last night? Some very interesting
matters were discussed there.—"What were they?"—
"Does a man who occupies another's premises, unknown
to the owner, have to pay rent or not?"—Under what
circumstances? If the premises were not for rent, and
the man who occupied them was not in the habit of renting places, we cannot say then that the owner sustained
a loss, or that the other derived a benefit. But if the
premises were for rent, and the other is in the practice of
renting places, then the owner sustained a loss and the
other derived a benefit. Then there is the case, where
the premises are not for rent, but the man who occupied
them is in the habit of renting places; the owner may say
you have derived a benefit, while the other may answer;
you have sustained no loss. Rami ben Hama said to
Rabbi Hisda: There is a *Mishna* that enlightens us on
this problem.—Which *Mishna?*—If you will render me
a service I shall tell you. Rabbi Hisda took his shawl
and folded it carefully. Then Rami ben Hama told him:
"If the animal derived a benefit the owner must pay
damages to the extent of the benefit." Raba remarked:
How little an opponent recognizes one's errors, if one
is lucky! This case is not at all similar to the one in
the *Mishna*, but Rab Hisda accepted it. In that case
one derives a benefit and the other sustains a loss, but
here one derives a benefit while the other sustains no
loss. Rami ben Hama: How did he arrive at this conclusion? He was of the opinion that if one leaves produce in a public place, he probably gave up the title to it.

(*Gemara*)

A HUMAN being is considered a danger at all times, whether he causes damage unwittingly or deliberately, whether awake or asleep. If a man has blinded his neighbor's eye, or ruined any utensils, he must pay full damages.   (*Mishna*)

FROM CHAPTER II

IF A man pours out water into a public place and someone is injured by it, he is liable for damages. If a man hides thorns or glass, or has made his fence of thorns, or if the fence has fallen into a public street, and someone is injured by it, he is liable for damages.

If a man put his straw and his stubble into a public place in order to make manure of it, and someone is injured by it, he is liable for the damage; and whoever comes first may appropriate the straw. Rabbi Gamaliel said: Whoever clutters up a public place, and thereby causes damage to anyone, he is liable for it, and whoever comes first may appropriate what was left there. If a man has turned up manure in a public place, and someone was injured by it, he is liable for the damage. (*Mishna*)

MAY we infer that the *Mishna* is not in accord with the view of Rabbi Yehuda? For we learned that Rabbi Yehuda said that during the season when manure is prepared, a man may put out his dung into the public street, so that men and beasts will tread upon it, for with this understanding Joshua made the land available to the people.—But you may say that Rabbi Yehuda concurs in this, for he too maintains that if damage is caused, restitution must be made for the damage.

(*Gemara*)

IF A man walked carrying a barrel and another came
carrying a beam, and the barrel was broken by the beam,
the man with the beam is not liable, for both have the
right of way. If the man with the beam came first, and
the man with the barrel came behind him, and the barrel
was broken by the beam, he is not liable. But if the
man with the beam stopped suddenly; he is liable, but if
he warned the man with the barrel to stop, he is not liable. If the man with the barrel came first, and the man
with the beam was behind him, and the barrel was
broken by the beam; the man with the beam is liable, but
if the man with the barrel stopped, he is not liable; but
if the first man said to the beam carrier, Stop, the man
with the beam is liable. This applies to one who comes
carrying a candle, while another comes carrying flax.

If a man splits wood in private premises and injures
someone in a public thoroughfare, or if he is doing it in a
public thoroughfare and injures someone on private
property, or if he is on private property and injures
someone on another private property, he is liable.

There are instances when a man may be liable for the
acts of his ox, but not liable for his own acts, and then
there are instances when a man may be liable for his
own acts, but not for those of his ox. If his ox caused
indignity, he is not liable, but if the man himself caused
indignity, he is liable. If a man's ox blinded the eye of
his slave, or knocked out his tooth, he is not liable, but if
he himself blinded the eye of his slave or knocked out
his tooth, he is liable. If an ox injured his father or
his mother, he is liable, but if he himself injured his
father or his mother, he is not liable. If an ox set fire to
a stack of corn on the Sabbath, he is liable; but if the

man himself set fire to a stack of corn on the Sabbath, he is not liable for damages, for in those cases he is subject to capital punishment.

If one ox was running after another ox, and either was found to be injured, and one owner says: Your ox injured my ox, and the other says: No, it was injured by a stone, the burden of proof rests with the one who wants to exact the payment.   (*Mishna*)

SAID Rabbi Hiya ben Abba. Here the colleagues of Symachus disagreed with him, for he maintained that money the ownership of which could not be ascertained should be equally divided between the two contestants. Said Rabbi Abba ben Memel to Rabbi Hiya ben Abba: Did Symachus express the same opinion in a case where both contestants claimed that they were positive of the ownership of the money involved? Yes, he answered. Symachus adhered to this opinion even where both contestants claimed to be certain to whom the money ought to go. But how do you know that the *Mishna* is treating here of a case where both contestants are positive of the claim?—Because it states: One says your ox caused the injury, while the other says, no.   (*Gemara*)

FROM CHAPTER IV

IF A potter brings his pots into the courtyard of a householder without the permission of the owner, and the householder's beast breaks them, the householder is not liable. If the beast is injured by the pots, the potter is liable; but if he brings in the pots by permission, then the householder is liable. If he brings his produce into the courtyard of the householder without permission, and the householder's cattle eat it, the householder is exempt from payment, and if the cattle are harmed by it, the owner of the produce is liable. But if he brings it in by permission, then the owner of the courtyard is liable.

If a man brings his ox into the courtyard of a householder without permission, and an ox belonging to the householder gores it, or his dog bites it, the householder is exempt from paying for the damage. But if it gores an ox belonging to the householder, then the man who brought in the ox is liable. If the ox falls into the householder's well and pollutes its water, the owner of the ox is liable. If the father or the son of the householder is in the well, and is killed by the ox, the owner must pay the ransom price. But if he brings in the ox with the permission of the householder, then the owner of the courtyard is liable. Rabbi says: The householder is never liable unless he agrees to watch over the property that is brought in.   (*Mishna*)

THE Rabbis taught: If the householder says: Bring in your ox and watch it, and if the ox causes damage, the owner of the ox would be liable. But should the ox be injured, the owner of the yard would not be liable. If, however, the householder said: Bring in your ox and I will watch it, then if the ox should be injured the householder is liable, but should the ox cause any damage, its owner would be exempt from paying for the damage.

There is here a contradiction: At first you argue: If the owner said: Bring in your ox and watch it, and if the ox should cause damage, the owner would be liable, but should the ox be injured the householder would not be liable. The reason for this is that he plainly says to

the owner of the ox: watch it. Thus the owner of the
ox is liable, and the householder is exempt. From this
we may infer that if no mention was made of watching
the ox, the owner of the yard would be liable, and the
owner of the ox exempt. In other words by keeping
silent the householder indicates that he will watch the ox.
Now the following text reads: If he said: Bring in your
ox and I will watch it, then should the ox be injured,
the householder would be liable, but should it cause damage the owner of it would be exempt. The reason is
that the householder plainly said: "I will watch it." From
this we infer, if the householder kept silent, the owner
of the ox would be liable and the householder would be
exempt. For in this case there is no indication that the
householder will watch the ox. This is in accord with
Rabbi who said, that there is no liability on the part of
the householder unless he agreed to watch over the ox.
Is then the first clause according to the Rabbis and the
concluding one according to Rabbi? Rabbi Eleazar said:
The contradiction is quite obvious: whoever taught the
first, did not teach the second. Raba however explained: The entire text can be taken as in accord with
the Rabbis: since in the first part we learn: "watch it"
in the second part we learn: "I will watch it." Rab
Papa explained: The whole text is in accord with Rabbi,
for he concurred here with the opinion of Rabbi Tarfon
who said: For the damages caused by "Horn" on private ground, the owner of the ox is liable for full damages. It therefore indicates, that where he plainly says:
"watch it" he did not transfer to him any rights to any
part of the property, so that it comes under the rule of a
Horn causing damage on private property, and thus the

liability is for full damage. Where, however, he did not plainly say: "watch it" he, it is assumed, granted him the right to some place on his property, so that this would come under the ruling of the "Horn" causing damage on property of joint ownership, and the liability, here, is of payment for half damages.   (*Gemara*)

IF A man digs a pit on public property and an ox or an ass fall into it, he is liable for the damage caused. . . .

If a pit belonged to two partners and one passed over it and did not cover it, and the second partner did not cover it either, the second is held liable. If the first one covered it, but the second found it open and did not cover it, the second is liable. If he covered it properly, and an ox or an ass fell into it, he is exempt, but if he did not cover it properly, and an ox or an ass fell into it and was killed, he is liable.   (*Mishna*)

FROM CHAPTER V

IF A man left his cattle in the sun, or he entrusted them to the care of a deaf-mute, an imbecile, or a minor, and they came out and caused damage, he is liable. If he entrusted his flock to a shepherd, the shepherd takes the place of the owner. If the flock got into a garden and derived a benefit from it, the owner of the flock pays for the amount of benefit that it derived. If they went by it in the usual way and caused damage, he pays for the damage. How does he pay for the damage? They estimate how much a *seah's* space of ground in the field was worth before, and how much it is worth now. Rabbi Simon says: If the cattle ate ripe fruit, he must pay for ripe fruit. If they damaged one *seah* the owner of the flock shall pay one *seah,* if two, he shall pay two.

(*Mishna*)

RABBI Joshua said: There are four things for which a man who commits them is exempt from the judgment of men, but is guilty before the judgment of Heaven: And these are the following: He that knocks down a fence in front of his neighbor's cattle; he that bends his neighbor's stacks of corn towards a fire; he that hires false witnesses, and he that knows of testimony favorable to his neighbor, and does not testify.

(*Gemara*)

IF A man caused a fire through a deaf-mute, an imbecile, or a minor, he is not liable under the laws of man, but he is guilty under the laws of Heaven, but if he caused a fire through a person of sound judgment, that person is liable. If one brought the fire, and then another brought the wood, the one who brought the wood is liable. If one brought the wood, then another brought the fire, the one who brought the fire is liable. If a third person came and fanned the flames, he is liable, but if the wind fanned the flame, all are exempt.

(*Mishna*)

SAID Rabbi Simon ben Lakish in the name of Hezekiah: This interpretation refers only to the man who handed to one of these a coal, and that one fanned it; but if he handed one a blazing flame, he is liable. What is the reason? It was his action that caused the fire. But Rabbi Yohanan said: Even if he handed one a blazing flame, he is not liable. What is the reason? The reason is that the actions of the deaf-mute caused the fire. He is not liable unless he supplied him with wood, shavings, and a light, for in that case it is a certainty that it was his deed that caused the fire.

RABBI Ammi and Rabbi Assi were sitting before Rabbi Isaac the smith. One asked him to give them a talk on some legal point while the other asked for a homiletic exposition. When he wanted to discourse on something homiletic, the first would not let him; and when he tried to talk about some legal point, the other would not let him. He said to them: I will tell you a parable. To what can this be likened? To a man who had two wives, one young and one old; the young would pull out his white hair, while the old would pull out his black hair, so that he finally became entirely bald. Whereupon he said to them: I shall tell you something that will be of interest to both of you: (*Exodus* xxii, 6) *If a fire breaks out, and catch thorns,* (breaks out means "of itself") *he that kindled the fire shall surely make restitution.* The Holy One, blessed be He, said: I ought to make restitution for the fire that I had kindled in Zion, for it was said: (*Lament.* iv, 11) *And hath kindled a fire in Zion, and it hath devoured the foundations thereof,* and some day I shall rebuild it with fire, for it was said: (*Zechariah* ii, 5) *For I, saith the Lord, will be unto her a wall of fire round about, and will be the glory in the midst of her.* The legal viewpoint: The verse begins with damages caused by a chattel and concludes with damage caused by a person. This is to enlighten us that fire means also a human agency.

A man once kicked another man's money-box into the river. The owner came and said: I had such-and-such valuables in it. Rabbi Ashi sat and pondered the problem. How should he decide in a case of this kind? Whereupon Rabina said to Rabbi Aha ben Raba, or as some say, it was Rabbi Aha ben Raba who said it to Rabbi Ashi: Is not this the same as what we learned in the *Mishna?* There we learned: "The Sages agree with Rabbi Yehuda, that when a man sets fire to a house, he must make restitution for everything that was in it, for it is customary for people to keep their property in their homes." He replied: If he had asked for money that he kept there, it would have come under the same ruling. However, in this case, the man contends that he had jewels in the box. How shall I decide? Do people keep jewels in their money boxes or not?—This remained without decision.   *(Gemara)*

FROM CHAPTER VI

THERE are more cases of two fold payments than payments of four-fold and five-fold. For two-fold payments apply to things that are alive and to those that have no life in them, while four-fold and five-fold payments apply only to an ox or a sheep, for it was said: (*Exodus* xxii, 1) *If a man shall steal an ox, or a sheep, and kill it, or sell it; he shall restore five oxen for an ox and four sheep for a sheep.* If one steals from a thief he does not have to make two-fold restitution, and if one slaughters or sells what he steals from a thief, he does not have to make four-fold or five-fold payments.

Small cattle must not be raised in the Land of Israel, but one may raise them in Syria and in the deserts that

are in the Land of Israel. One must not breed fowls in
Jerusalem because of the Holy Places, but priests must
not do so anywhere in the land, because of uncleanliness.
Pigs must not be bred anywhere. A man must not raise
a dog unless he keeps him on a chain. One must not
place traps for pigeons within thirty *ris* from an inhabited place.   (*Mishna*)

THE Rabbis taught: If a shepherd repents, he must
not be compelled to sell all at once, but he shall sell a
few at a time. The same applies to a proselyte who in-
herited dogs and pigs, he must not be compelled to sell
them all at once, but sell them a few at a time. The same
is with a man who has vowed to buy a house, or marry
a wife in the Land of Israel, he does not have to act
upon his vow at once, but he may wait till he finds what
suits him. There was a case of a woman whose son was
annoying her. In exasperation she vowed: Whoever will
offer to marry me, I shall not refuse him. Men who
were not suitable presented themselves to her with an
offer of marriage. The matter was laid before the Sages.
They declared: This woman, surely, did not intend to
marry anyone that was not suitable for her.

RAB, and Samuel, and Rabbi Assi once went to a cir-
cumcision and some say it was a birthday celebration.
Rab would not enter before Samuel, and Samuel would
not enter before Rabbi Assi, and Rabbi Assi would not
enter before Rab, and so they stood there arguing who
should enter last. It was finally decided that Samuel
should wait, while Rab and Rabbi Assi should go in.
Rab yielded his precedence out of deference to Samuel
to whom he wanted to show honor, because of that sad

occasion, when he had once uttered a curse against him.
In the meantime a cat came by and bit the hand of a
child. Whereupon Rab in his lecture declared: "It is
permitted to kill a cat, and one must not keep it. And
furthermore the laws of theft, or the return of a lost
object to its owner do not apply to it. . . ."

Rabbi Simon ben Eleazar said: One may keep village dogs, cats, monkeys, and porcupines, because they
help to keep the house clean. There is no contradiction
here. One refers to a black cat, while the other refers
to a white cat. But was not the biting in Rab's case
caused by a black cat?—Yes, it was a black cat, but it
was the offspring of a white one. Is not this the case
of which Rabina raised a question? For Rabina asked:
What should be the ruling in case of a black cat that was
an offspring of a white one?—The question asked by
Rabina was in reference to a black cat that was the offspring of a white one which in turn was an offspring of
a black one. The case of which Rab spoke was that of a
black cat which was the offspring of a white one which in
turn was an offspring of another white cat.

THE Rabbis taught: Joshua the son of Nun made ten
stipulations: The cattle may graze in the woods; wood
may be gathered in anybody's field, grasses may also be
gathered in any place, except in the field of planted
clover; shoots may be cut in all places, except the stump
of the olive; a spring that has opened for the first time
may be used by all the inhabitants of a town; anyone
may fish in the sea of Tiberias, provided he does not
spread a sail, for this would hamper the boats; one may
relieve himself against any fence, even a fence that en-

closes a field of saffron; anyone may use the paths in a private field, till the time of the second rains; anyone is permitted to use the sides of the road because of obstructions on the main road; if one is lost in a vineyard, he may cut his way through when going up or down; and a corpse that is found acquires the right to be buried on the spot.

Ezra has enacted ten acts: That the *Torah* be read on the Sabbath at the afternoon services, that on Mondays and Thursdays the *Torah* should also be read, that court be held on Mondays and Thursdays, that washing should be done on Thursdays, that garlic should be eaten on Sabbath eve, that housewives rise early and bake, that a woman should wear a *sinar*, that a woman should comb her hair before she enters the public bath, that peddlers of spices may travel through the towns; and he also enacted that those who were polluted be required to cleanse themselves.   (*Gemara*)

FROM CHAPTER VII

IF A man injures his fellow he is liable to him for five things: for damage, for pain, for medical treatment, for loss of time, and for indignity. How, for damage?—If he blinded him or cut off his hand, or broke his leg, the injured is looked upon as if he were a slave, that is being sold in the market. How much was he worth before, and how much is he worth now? How, for pain?—If he burned him with a spit or a nail, even though it were only on his fingernails, where it does not cause a wound; it is estimated how much money a man of equal standing would be willing to take to suffer that much. How, for medical treatment? If he struck him he must pay for the medical treatment, if ulcers developed, if it is a result of the inflicted wound, he is liable, but if not, he is exempt. If it opened and was healed and then reopened again, he must pay for the treatments, but if it was once healed completely, he does not become liable again. Loss of time?—He is looked upon as if he were a watchman of a field of cucumbers, for he has already been paid the value of his hand or his leg. Indignity?—All depends on the standing of the man who inflicted the indignity, and the person who suffered the indignity. If a man inflicted indignity on a naked person, on a blind person, or on a sleeping one, he is liable. But if the man was asleep while doing it, he is exempt. If a man fell from a roof and thereby injured and inflicted indignity upon someone, he is liable for the injury, but not for the indignity. A man is not liable for indignity unless he inflicted it with intention. (*Mishna*)

HOW then? It is written: (*Exodus* xxi, 24) *Eye for an eye.* Does not the All-Merciful actually mean the eye? Let this enter your mind. For we learned: One would believe, that if one blinded a fellow's eye, the offender's eye would be blinded, or if he cut off his arm, the offender's arm would be cut off, or if he broke his leg, the offender's leg would be broken. Therefore it was stated: (*Leviticus* xxiv, 17, 18) *And he that killeth any man shall surely be put to death. And he that killeth a beast shall make it good; beast for beast.* Just as for the smiting of a beast a money payment is made, so also in case he smiteth a man, money should be paid for the damage. But if you would wish to contend otherwise:— why it was said: (*Numbers* xxxv, 31) *Moreover ye shall take no satisfaction for the life of a murderer, which is guilty of death.* This means that for the life of a murderer payment may not be accepted, but for a limb that cannot grow black, we may accept payment. (*Gemara*)

THE law, here, is more severe for man than for the ox. A man must pay for injury, pain, medical treatment, loss of time, indignity and the value of the unborn child, but in the case of an ox there is no payment but only for damage caused, and there is also exemption for the value of the unborn child.

If a man strikes his fellow, he must pay him a *selah*. Rabbi Yehuda says, in the name of Rabbi Yosi the Galilean, that he pays him a *maneh*. If he slaps his face, he pays two hundred *zuz*; if he slaps his face with the back of his hand, he pays him four hundred *zuz*.

If he tore his ear, or pulled his hair, or he spit at him and the saliva reached him, if he removed his clothing from him, if he uncovered a woman's head in the market place: he pays four hundred *zuz*. This is the general rule; it all depends upon the standing of the person injured. Rabbi Akiba said: Even the poorest in Israel are looked upon as free men who have lost their fortunes, for they are the children of Abraham, Isaac, and Jacob.

It once happened that a man uncovered the head of a woman in the market place. She came before Rabbi Akiba, who ordered the offender to pay her four hundred *zuz*. The man asked for time in which to make the payment, and Rabbi Akiba granted him time. The man then watched the woman until he saw her standing at the entrance of her yard. Before her eyes he broke a jar containing an *isar* of oil. She uncovered her head, scooped up the oil in her hand and put it to her head. He then brought witnesses to this affair, and came before Rabbi Akiba and asked: To such a woman must I pay four hundred *zuz*? Rabbi Akiba answered: You have made no point. If a man should wound himself, though he has no right to do so, he is exempt, but if another person wounds him, that other is liable.

Though a person pays for the injury, he is not forgiven, till he begs forgiveness from the injured person.

If a man says: Blind my eye, or cut off my arm, or break my leg, the man that does it is guilty. Even if the man said: I agree that you won't be liable, the other is still guilty. If he says: Tear my garments, or break my jar, the other man is liable; and if he said to him: I agree that you won't be liable, he is still liable, whether he injured the person or his property.   (*Mishna*)

FROM CHAPTER VIII

IF ONE steals wood and makes articles of it, or he steals wool and makes garments of it, he pays for them according to their value at time of the theft. If one stole a cow that was pregnant, and it gave birth, or a sheep with wool, and he sheared it, he pays the value of a cow about to give birth, or the value of a sheep ready to be sheared. If he stole a cow which became pregnant in his possession and then gave birth, or a sheep which grew its wool while in his possession, and then sheared it, he pays according to the value at the time of the theft. This is the rule: All robbers pay in accordance with the value of the property at the time of the robbery.

(*Mishna*)

THE Rabbis taught: If robbers or usurers are willing to return property, one does not accept it from
them, and if he does, he does it against the wishes of the
Sages. Rabbi Yohanan said: This doctrine was inaugurated at the time of Rabbi. Once a certain man wanted
to repent and return stolen property, whereupon his wife
said to him: You fool! If you begin to make restitution,
even the girdle that you are wearing belongs to another,
so he stopped and did not repent. It was then inaugurated that if robbers and usurers are ready to repent
and return property, it is not proper to accept it from
them; and whoever accepts it, does so against the wishes
of the Sages.

Come and hear: Robbers and usurers, even if they
have already collected the mony, must make restitution.
—What has a robber to collect? They either robbed,
or they did not rob—Rather read: Robbers, that is to
say usurers, even if they have already collected the
money, must make restitution. I will tell you, they must
make restitution, but one does not accept it from them.
Then why must they make restitution?—So as to fulfill
their duty before Heaven.

Come and hear: For shepherds, tax collectors, and
revenue contractors it is very hard to repent but still they
must make restitution to those they know that they have
robbed.   (*Gemara*)

FROM CHAPTER IX

IF A man stole things and fed them to his children,
or left it to them upon his death, they are exempt from
making restitution. But if it is mortgagable property,
they must make restitution.   (*Mishna*)

RAB said: The law is that a document of indebtedness can be attested even though the defendant is not present, or even if he is present and proclaims aloud that it is a forgery. But if he pleads for time to bring witnesses and disprove the document, he must be given the necessary time. If he appears, well and good, but if he does not appear, then we wait till Monday, and Thursday and another Monday. If he still does not appear, we issue a warrant against him returnable in ninety days. For the first thirty days we don't take possession of his property for we take it that he is trying to borrow the money; for the next thirty days we do not take his property—we think he might not have been able to raise a loan and is now trying to sell the property, for the last thirty days we still do not seize his property for we take it that the buyer is now busy raising the purchase money. It is after he has not appeared all this time that we issue an order of execution for the seizure of the property. This procedure takes place only if he pleaded for time, but if he said: "I will not appear", an order for the seizure of the property is issued at once. An order of seizure can be issued only on real estate, but not on movable property, because the creditor can take away the movable property and dispose of it, and should the defendant later appear with witnesses to prove the document faulty, he would find naught which he could recover.   (Gemara)

ONE does not take change from the box of a taxgatherer or the purse of a tax collector, nor may one accept charity from them; but one may accept it in their own homes or in the market place.

If tax-gatherers took a man's ass and gave him another ass, or if robbers took his cloak and gave him another cloak, he may keep them, because the original owner has given up all hope of recovery.

One must not buy from shepherds wool or milk or kids, nor fruits or wood from gardeners, but in Judea one may buy woolen articles from women, and in Galilee one may buy flax, and in Sharon one may buy calves. But if a person sell any of these on condition that it be kept hidden, it is forbidden to buy. Eggs and chickens may be bought anywhere.   (*Mishna*)

THE Rabbis taught: From shepherds one must not buy goats or kids or fleece, nor shreds of wool; but one may buy from them sewn garments, as these are surely their own. In the desert one may buy from them milk and cheese, but not in inhabited places. It is further permissible to buy from them four or five sheep, or four or five fleeces, but one must not buy two sheep or two fleeces. Rabbi Yehuda says: Domestic animals one may buy from them, but undomesticated one must not buy. This is the rule: All things that a shepherd sells that would be noticed by his master are permissible; but those that might not be noticed by his master are forbidden.

One may buy fruit from the gardeners if they are offering it for sale while seated before their baskets with their scales in front of them, but under no circumstances should one buy if one is told to hide it. One may also buy fruit from them in front of the garden, but not in back of it.   (*Gemara*)

FROM CHAPTER X

Law of Procedure

ASES concerning money matters are decided by three judges. Cases of larceny and injury by three judges. Damages, half damages, double, four-fold or five-fold payments by three judges. The violator, the seducer, and the slanderer are judged by three. Thus, according to Rabbi Meir; but the Sages say: Cases of libel should be judged by twenty-three judges, because they may involve capital punishment. Cases punishable by flogging are judged by three, but according to Rabbi Ishmael they should be judged by twenty-three. . . . Redemption of sacred property by three; Rabbi Yehuda says: One of the judges should be a priest. Real estate by nine and a priest.

Cases involving capital punishment are judged by twenty-three, as are cases of beasts and men who commit unnatural intercourse.

The ox that is to be stoned, by twenty-three, for it was said: (*Leviticus* xxi, 29) *The ox shall be stoned and its owner shall be put to death.* Those that have jurisdiction over the owner of the ox shall judge the ox. The

wolf, the lion, the bear, the leopard, the panther, or the
serpent,—their death is decided by twenty-three judges.
A tribe, a false prophet, or a High Priest is judged by a
court of seventy-one.

An offensive war is not to be declared, except by the
authority of a court of seventy-one.

The Great Sanhedrin shall consist of seventy-one,
while the Small Sanhedrin shall consist of twenty-
three.   (*Mishna*)

RABBI Aha ben Rabbi Ika says: According to the
Torah, every one is competent to pass on cases of indebtedness, for it was said: (*Leviticus* xix, 15) *In righteousness thou shalt judge thy neighbor.* But three are required, since they are laymen. For it is not likely that
no one of the three should have no knowledge whatsoever of law.

The Rabbis taught: Cases of money are decided by
three. Rabbi says by a vote of five, so that a majority
decision may be rendered by three. But when three sit
can't there be a verdict rendered by a majority of two?
What Rabbi evidently meant was that there must be a
concurring decision of at least three. Rabbi Abahu
poked fun at this: in that case the Great Sanhedrin
would have to be composed of one hundred and forty-
one, so that a majority decision of seventy-one could be
rendered, and the Small Sanhedrin would have to be
composed of forty-five, so that a majority decision of
twenty-three could be rendered. But this is not so. The
Merciful said: (*Numbers* xi, 16) *Gather unto me seventy
men, of the elders of Israel.* Seventy at the time of
gathering.

The Rabbis taught: Monetary cases are judged by three, but if one is an experienced judge, he may render a decision alone. Rabbi Nahman said: One, like me, may render a decision alone in a case involving money. And so said Rabbi Hiya.

Come and hear: Mar Zutra the son of Rabbi Nahman judged a case and rendered an erroneous decision. He came before Rabbi Joseph who told him: If both litigants accepted you as their judge, you are not liable, but if not, go and make restitution to the loser. From this it can be inferred that the decision of an unauthorized judge is also valid.

Rab said: If one wishes to judge monetary cases alone, and does not wish to incur liability, he must receive authorization from the Exilarch. And thus said Rabbi Samuel also.

Rabbi Samuel ben Mansya said: If two litigants come before you, before you have heard their case, or if you have heard it, and have not decided to which side the verdict inclines, you may tell them: Go and compromise; but if you have heard their case and have made up your mind as to the verdict, you must not tell them to settle it by a compromise.

THE Rabbis taught: The calendar cannot be set save by a court especially appointed for that purpose.

There was the case of Rabbi Gamaliel who ordered: Send up seven scholars to my upper chamber for this purpose. When he came he found that there were eight. He asked who came here without authorization? Whereupon Samuel the Little arose and said: I am the one who came up here without authorization, but I have come

not to intercalate the year but to learn how the law is
applied in practice. Said Rabbi Gamaliel: You may sit
down, my son. You are worthy that every year shall be
intercalated by you. The Sages, however, decided that
the year may be lengthened only by a court appointed
specifically for that purpose.—But it was really not Samuel the Little that had come unauthorized, but another.
But because he did not want to shame the other fellow,
he arose.

IT HAPPENED once that while Rabbi was lectur-
ing he smelled garlic. He said: Whoever ate garlic, let
him leave the room. Whereupon Rabbi Hiya arose and
left the room. Then all the other disciples arose one
after the other and left the room. Next morning Rabbi
Hiya met Rabbi Simon, the son of Rabbi, and was asked:
Are you the one that annoyed my father yesterday? He
answered: A thing like this should never occur in Israel.

From whom did Rabbi Hiya learn to act like this?—
From Rabbi Meir. It was related that a woman came
once to the academy of Rabbi Meir and said to him:
Rabbi, one of you betrothed me through intercourse.
Whereupon the Rabbi arose, wrote out a writ of divorce,
and handed it to her. Thereupon all the disciples arose
and each in his turn gave her a writ of divorce.

The Rabbis taught: A year may not be intercalated
unless it is necessary for the improvement of roads or
the strengthening of bridges, or the repair of the ovens
for the Paschal Offering. Or because of the Pilgrims
who have left their homes, but have not yet arrived;
but not because of the snows or the cold, or the Pilgrims
who have not as yet set out from their homes.

RABBI Yohanan said: Only such are selected for the Sanhedrin as possess stature, appearance, wisdom; and are ripe in years; as have a knowledge of sorcery, and understand seventy languages, so that the Sanhedrin will not have to employ interpreters.

Rabbi Yehuda said, in the name of Rab: In the city where one cannot find two men who speak seventy languages and one who understands them, no Sanhedrin should be appointed there. In the city of Bethar there were three such men, and in Yabnah four: Rabbi Eliezer, Rabbi Joshua, Rabbi Akiba, and Simon the Yemenite, who would discourse while sitting before his masters on the floor.   (*Gemara*)

FROM CHAPTER I

THE High Priest may judge and may be judged. He may testify and others may testify against him. *Halizah* may be performed upon him, and one may submit to *Halizah* by his widow. He cannot contract levirate marriage, for as a Priest he is forbidden to marry a widow. If someone dies in his family, he must not follow the bier. If the bier appears within his sight he must disappear. But he may follow the procession to the gates of the city. Thus according to Rabbi Meir; but Rabbi Yehuda says: He does not venture out of the Temple.

The King does not judge, and no one judges him. He does not testify and one cannot testify against him. He does not submit to *Halizah,* nor does his wife perform the rite to anyone. He does not contract levirate marriage, nor does anyone contract levirate marriage with his widow. Rabbi Yehuda says: If the King is willing to submit to *Halizah*, or is willing to contract levirate marriage, he merits praise.   (*Mishna*)

"THE High Priest may judge." Is not this quite obvious? This is stated so that we may adduce that he may be judged. But this too is obvious. For how could he judge if he cannot be judged? For it was written: (*Zephania* ii, 1) *Gather yourselves together, yea, gather together.* And Resh-Lakish explained: Adorn thyself and then adorn others. Further we are taught: A King does not judge, and no one judges a King, so he also teaches: "The High Priest may judge and may be judged." But if you wish, we may say that what we are taught is really the following lesson: If a High Priest killed anyone intentionally, he is sentenced to death, but if he killed anyone unintentionally, he is exiled. If he transgresses a positive or a negative command, in either case, he receives the same treatment as any ordinary person.

The Rabbis said: Originally the mourner used to stand, while the people passed by, but two families in Jerusalem fought with each other over the privilege of passing first. So the Rabbis instituted the custom of the people standing while the mourners pass by.

"The King does not judge", etc. Rabbi Joseph said: This refers only to the Kings of Israel, but the Kings of the House of David may judge and may be judged. For it was written: (*Jeremiah* xxi, 12) *Oh House of David, thus said the Lord; Execute judgment in the morning.* And if the King could not be judged, how could he judge others? Was it not written "Gather and be gathered" which, as Resh-Lakish explained, meant "Adorn thyself and then adorn others?" But why not the Kings of Israel? Because of the case of a slave of King Yanai who once killed a man. Simon ben Shetah said to the Sages: Mark the man, and we shall take him to court. They sent word to the King saying: "Your slave has killed a man." He sent the slave to them. They sent word to him: "Thou too must come", for the law says: (*Exodus* xxi, 29) *If it hath been testified to his owners.* The owner of the ox must come and stand by his ox. The King came to court and sat down. Then Simon ben Shetah said to him: Stand on thy feet, King Yanai, and let the witnesses testify against thee. Thou art not standing before us, but before Him who spoke and the world was created, art thou standing. As it was written: (*Deuteronomy* xix, 17) *Then both the men, between whom the controversy is, shall stand before the Lord.* Said the King, "I shall not do as thou sayest, but as thy colleagues say". Simon then turned to his right and saw that they all were looking to the ground. He turned to the left and saw that there, too, all were looking to the ground. Said Simon ben Shetah to them, "Are all of you engrossed in thought? Then let the Master of thought come and call you to account". Instantly Gabriel appeared and smote them to the ground, and they died. Right there and then it was decreed that a King does not judge, and no one judges a King. He does not testify, and no one may testify against him.

(Gemara)

THE King may set forth to a voluntary war only upon the decision of a court of seventy-one. He has right of domain to establish a road through private property and no one may protest against him. The King's road has no limit. Whatever the people plunder, they must set before him and he takes the first portion.

No one may ride on the King's horse, nor sit on his throne, and no one may make use of his sceptre. No one may gaze upon him while he is having his hair cut, or when he is naked, or when he is in the bath house. For it was said: (*Deuteronomy* xvii, 15) *Thou shalt in everywise set him King over thee. His awe shall be over thee.*   (*Mishna*)

RAB Yehuda said in the name of Samuel: All that is said in the chapter of the King, the King may do. Rab said: This whole chapter was brought forth only for the purpose of inspiring awe for him among the people.

MAR Zutra, and some say it was Mar Ukba, said: Originally the *Torah* was given to the Israelites in Hebrew script and in the Holy Hebrew tongue. Later it was given to them, in the day of Ezra, in the Assyrian script and in the Aramaic tongue. The Israelites then selected the Assyrian script and the Holy tongue, and left the Hebrew script and the Aramaic language for the laymen.

RABBI Jacob said in the name of Rabbi Yohanan: Abishag was allowed to be married to King Solomon, but she was not allowed to Adoniyah. She was allowed to Solomon because he was King, and the King may make use of the King's sceptre. But she was not allowed to Adoniyah because he was an ordinary citizen.

Said Rabbi Shaman ben Aba: See how hard divorcing was made! King David was allowed to marry Abishag, but he was not allowed to divorce any of his wives.

Rabbi Eliezer said: When a man divorces his wife, even the altar sheds tears for him.

Rabbi Alexandri said: A man whose wife dies while he is alive, is as if the world darkened about him.

Rabbi Samuel ben Nahman said: Everything can be replaced but the wife of one's youth. For it was said: (*Isaiah* liv, 6) *And a wife of youth, when thou wast refused.*

Rab Yehuda lectured his son Isaac: A man finds joy only with his first wife. For it was said: (*Prov.* v, 18) *Let thy fountain be blessed: and rejoice with the wife of thy youth.* (*Gemara*)

FROM CHAPTER II

MONETARY cases are judged by three; each litigant selects one judge and then both together select one. Thus says Rabbi Meir, but the Sages say: The two judges select a third. Each litigant may reject the judge selected by the other. Thus says Rabbi Meir. But the Sages say: The judges may be rejected only if they are related to a litigant or are otherwise disqualified. But if the judges are eligible or are experts they cannot be rejected. Each may reject the witnesses of the other. Thus says Rabbi Meir, but the Sages say: A witness may be rejected if he is a relative or otherwise ineligible, but if they are eligible they may not be disqualified.

The following are ineligible: dice-players, usurers, pigeon-fliers, and dealers in produce of the seventh year. (*Mishna*)

WHAT sin does a dice player commit? Said Rammi
ben Hamma: Because the game is a speculation, and a
speculation cannot be binding by law, and thus he receives
ill-gotten money. Rabbi Shesheth said: It is not a question of speculation. The reason is, that gamblers are
not concerned with the welfare of the people.

Pigeon-fliers. Who is called a pigeon-flier? Here
it was explained: A man who says: If your pigeon over-
takes mine, you win.

Rabbi Nahman said: One who is suspected of incest
is eligible as a witness. Said Rabbi Shesheth: Rabbi,
he deserves forty lashes but is still eligible as a witness?
Said Raba: Rabbi Nahman admits that he is not eligible
as a witness in matrimonial cases. Rabina or Rab Papa
said: He is not eligible as a witness in a divorce case,
but he may be a witness where marriage is concerned.

(*Gemara*)

HOW are witnesses examined? They used to bring
them into a room and they admonished them. Then all
were sent out, but one, the eldest, was left, and he was
asked: How do you know that so-and-so is indebted to
so-and-so? If he answered: He told me "I am indebted
to him" or "So-and-so told me that he is indebted to him",
—it means nothing. He must say: In our presence he
admitted to him that he owes him two hundred *zuz*.
Then they bring in the second witness and he is examined. If they find that their statements agree, the judges
discuss the matter. If two say he is not guilty, and one
says he is guilty; then he is not guilty. If two say he
is guilty and one says he is not guilty, then he is guilty.

If one says, "Guilty" and one says, "Not Guilty", or if two say, "Guilty" or two say, "Not Guilty", and one says, "I have no opinion", they must add to the judges.

When the judges were finished with their work, the litigants were admitted and the senior judge would announce: "So-and-so, you are guilty", or "So-and-so, you are not guilty". And whence do we know that when one of the judges goes out he must not say: "I said 'Not guilty' but my colleagues said 'Guilty', what could I do? They were in the majority". Of such a one it was said: (*Lev.* xix, 16) *Thou shalt not go up and down as a tale-bearer among thy people.* And it was also said: (*Prov.* xi, 13) *A talebearer revealeth secrets.*   (*Mishna*)

FROM CHAPTER III

THE same procedure applies to capital cases as to monetary cases. For it was said: (*Lev.* xxiv, 22) *Ye shall have one manner of law.* What is the difference between monetary cases and capital cases? Monetary cases are judged by three, while capital cases are judged by twenty-three. Monetary cases can be opened for acquittal or for conviction, but capital cases must be opened with motions for acquittal and must not be opened with motions for conviction. Monetary cases may be decided by a majority of one for conviction or for acquittal, but capital cases may be decided for acquittal by a majority of one, but for conviction they must be decided by at least a majority of two. In monetary cases the decision may be reversed for either conviction or acquittal. But in capital cases, it may be reversed if a man was convicted but if he was acquitted, it cannot be reversed. In monetary cases everyone may argue for conviction or for acquittal, but in capital cases everyone may argue for acquittal, but not everyone may argue for conviction.

Everyone is eligible to try monetary cases, but not everyone is eligible to try capital cases, only priests, levites and Israelites who are worthy of contracting marriages with priests.   (*Mishna*)

RABBI Hanina said: According to the *Torah,* there is but one law, which applies alike to monetary and capital cases; and the methods of procedure as regards inquiry and investigation are the same. For it was written: (*Leviticus* xxiv, 22) *Ye shall have one manner of law.* But what is the reason that it was decided to have the procedure different in capital cases from that in monetary cases? It was done so that the door would not be locked for borrowers. Then if the judges should err they should not be held responsible.—Then surely the doors would be locked for the borrowers.

Raba said: The Mishna refers to cases of fines, while Rabbi Hanina refers to cases of loans and admissions.
                    (*Gemara*)

THE Sanhedrin was arranged like a half a circular threshing floor so that the judges could see one another, and the scribes of the court stand before them; one to the right and one to the left of them. They write down the testimony for conviction and for acquittal. Rabbi Yehuda said: Three scribes; one writes down the testimony for acquittal, one writes down the testimony for conviction, while the third writes down the testimony both for conviction and for acquittal.

Three rows of disciples of the Sages sat before

them; each one had his designated place. If an additional judge was needed they appointed one from the first row, and one of the second row took a place in the first, and one from the third row went to the second, while one from the public was selected and seated in the third row. He was not seated in the place of the former, but in a place that was proper for him.

How were witnesses admonished? In capital cases they brought them in and said to them: Perhaps what you want to say is only supposition or hearsay, or testimony from the mouth of an eye-witness or from a truthful person? Do you know that we shall search and inquire and examine you, and do you know that capital cases are not like monetary cases? In monetary cases a man can repay the money and the error be forgiven, but in capital cases the blood of the convicted and of his potential seed to the end of time are upon you.

Perhaps they will say: What do we want with all this trouble?—Was it not once said: (*Leviticus* v, 1) *And is a witness, whether he hath seen or known of it; if he do not utter it.* And if you should say: Why should we be guilty of the man's blood? Was it however not said: (*Prov.* xi, 10) *When the wicked perish, there is shouting.*   (*Mishna*)

THE Rabbis taught: What is supposition? The judge said to them: Perhaps it was like this: You saw a man pursuing another fellow into a ruin and you ran after him. You found a sword in his hand and blood trickling from it, and a murdered man was in the throes of death. If that is what you saw—you saw nothing.

Though the Sanhedrin was abolished after the de-

struction of the temple, the four methods of execution
were not abolished. How so? They surely were abolished.—The law of the four deaths was not abolished.
Those who merited death by stoning, died by falling
from a roof or by being trampled to death by wild beasts.
Those who merited death by fire, died by perishing in a
fire or by a bite from a serpent. Those who merited
death by the sword were either handed to the government or robbers beset and killed them. Those who merited death by strangulation, died by drowning in a river,
or by suffocating.

THE Rabbis taught: Man was created one. And why?
So that the heretics would not say: There are many
Lords in heaven. Another reason is that he was created thus for the sake of the righteous and the evil.
So that the righteous might not say, we are the children
of the righteous, and the evil might not say, we are the
children of the evil. Another explanation is that it was
done for the sake of the families, so that the families
might not quarrel one with another. Now that man was
created one, the families quarrel one with another; how
much more would they quarrel if there had been two
created.

The Rabbis taught: Man was created one to proclaim
the greatness of our Lord, the King of Kings, the Holy
One, blessed be He. For a man stamps many coins with
one mould, and each one resembles the other, but the
Holy One, blessed be He, stamps each man from the
mould of the first man, and not one resembles the other.

Rabbi Meir used to say: In three things a man differs
from his fellow man: In voice, in looks, and in mind. In

voice and in looks for the sake of avoiding incest, and in mind because of robbers and extortioners.

Man was created on Sabbath eve so that heretics might not say that the Holy One, blessed be He, had partners in the creation of the world. Another explanation is that if man gets over-haughty, he may be reminded that the smallest insect preceded him in creation.

ONCE the Emperor said to Rabbi Gamaliel: Your God is a thief. For it is written: (*Genesis* ii, 21) *And the Lord caused a deep sleep to fall upon Adam and he slept,* etc. The Emperor's daughter interrupted: "Leave him to me and I will answer him." Whereupon she said to the Emperor: "Let me have a duke." "What need have you of a duke?"—She answered: "Robbers came last night and took from us a silver chalice and left in its stead a gold one." Said the King: "I wish that they would come to us like that every day." "Was not Adam satisfied that they took a rib from him, and in its stead gave him a maid to wait upon him?" "Well", replied the King, "what I mean to say is that they could have taken the rib openly." She answered: "Give me a piece of raw meat." When the piece of meat was given to her she put it under her armpit. After a while she took it out and put it before the Emperor and said: "Eat of it." He answered: "It is disgusting." Whereupon she said: "Had they taken the rib openly from Adam, Eve would have been disgusting to Adam."

The Emperor said to Rabbi Gamaliel: I know what your God is doing in heaven and where he sits. Whereupon Rabbi Gamaliel sighed and seemed worried. What is the matter? asked the Emperor. Rabbi Gamaliel an-

swered: I have a son in the lands overseas, and I am
yearning for him. I wish you would tell me about him.
Do I know where he is? said the Emperor. Whereupon
Rabbi Gamaliel replied: What is going on upon this
earth you know not, yet you seem to know what goes
on in heaven.

The Emperor said once to Rabbi Gamaliel: "It is
written: (*Psalm* cxlvii, 4) *He telleth the number of the
stars*, etc. What is so remarkable about this? I too can
count the stars." Whereupon Rabbi Gamaliel put some
quinces into a sieve and spun it around and said to the
Emperor: "Count them."—"Hold them still", said the
Emperor.—"The stars in heaven are revolving, too", said
Rabbi Gamaliel.

Once the Emperor said to Rabbi Tanhum: "Let us
all become one people." "That is fine", said Rabbi Tanhum, "but we who are circumcised cannot become like
you. Therefore you must become circumcised, and become like us." The Emperor answered: "You spoke
well, but whoever wins in an argument with the Emperor
is thrown into the arena." Whereupon he was thrown
into the arena but he was not devoured. Then one of
the heretics said: "They did not eat him because they
are not hungry." So they threw the heretic in, and he
was devoured instantly.   (*Gemara*)

FROM CHAPTER IV

IF THE judges find that the witnesses agreed in their
evidence they begin with the arguments in favor of the
accused. If one of the witnesses arises and says: I have
something in favor of the accused, and then one of the
disciples arises and says: "I have something to argue

for his conviction," the disciple is silenced. But if one of the disciples says: "I have something in favor of the accused", he is told to come up and sit with the judges, and he remains there all day. If he has something pertinent to say, they listen to him. If the defendant arises and says, I have something to argue in my own defense, they listen to him, but make sure his words are pertinent to the case.

If they acquitted him, he is set free; but if they found him guilty, they hold the sentence over till the next day. During the day they gather in pairs, they eat little, and drink no wine the whole day, and they discuss the case all night long. The next morning they rise and go to court early. The one who voted for acquittal says: I voted for his acquittal and I stand now for his acquittal. The one who was for conviction says: I voted for his conviction and I still stand for his conviction. One who was for conviction may now favor acquittal, but one who voted for acquittal must not change his stand. If they erred in something, the two scribes remind them of it. If they acquitted him, he is set free; but if not, they take a vote. If twelve are for acquittal, while eleven are for conviction, he is acquitted. If twelve are for conviction and eleven are for acquittal, or even if eleven are for acquittal and eleven are for conviction, while one says I know not, they must add to the judges. How many do they add? By pairs till seventy-one. If thirty-six are for acquittal and thirty-five are for conviction, he is acquitted. If thirty-six are for conviction, while thirty-five are for acquittal, the two sides argue the case till one of those who voted for conviction sees his way to vote for the acquittal.   (*Mishna*)

RABBI Hisda said: If one says he killed him with a sword while another says he killed him with a dagger, the evidence is contradictory. If one says: His garments were white, while another says his garments were black, their evidence is not held contradictory.

This was objected to. "Certain" means "certain". If one says: He killed him with a sword, while another says he killed him with a dagger, or one said his garments were white; the evidence surely is not certain. Rabbi Hisda explained: This refers to garments with which a man was strangled, in which case they are in the same category as the sword and the dagger.

"The two sides discuss, etc." But if they cannot agree, Rabbi Aha says: He is set free. And thus said Rabbi Yohanan: He is set free. Said Rab Papa to Abaya: Then why did they not set him free in the first place? Said Abaya: Rabbi Yohanan explained that this is done, so that the court will not be adjourned in confusion. Some say that Rab Papa said to Abaya: Why add to the judges? Let the original court discharge him. To which Abaya answered: Rabbi Yosi is of your opinion. For we were taught: Rabbi Yosi says: Just as a court of seventy-one is not increased, thus we need not add to a court of twenty-three.   (*Gemara*)

FROM CHAPTER V

WHEN the trial is over, the guilty is brought out to be stoned. The place of stoning is situated outside the court house. For it was said: (*Lev.* xxiv, 14) *Bring forth him that hath cursed.* One man stands at the door with a scarf in his hand, while another man sits on a horse in the distance but so that the man at the door can

see him. If someone comes and says: I have something
in favor of the condemned, the man at the door waves
the scarf and the horseman runs and stops the condemned. Even if the condemned says: I have something to say in my favor, he is brought back to court.
Even if it is four or five times, he is brought back, provided he has something pertinent to the case.

(Mishna)

"ONE man stands, etc." It is very clear that the stone
with which a man is to be stoned, the gallows on which
a man is to be hanged, and the sword with which he
is to be put to death or the cloth with which he is to
be strangled are all furnished by the community. Indeed, one cannot say to the condemned that he should
furnish the necessary things and put himself to death.
But then Rab Huna asked: Who furnishes the scarf
and the horse? These are for the purpose of saving the
man. Or should they be furnished at the expense of the
court, since the court is duty bound to endeavor to save
him? Furthermore, said Rabbi Hiya ben Ashi in the
name of Rab Hisda: When a man is led out to be executed he is to be given a cup of drugged wine so as to
becloud his spirit. For it was said: (*Prov.* xxxi, 6) *Give
strong drink unto him that is ready to perish, and wine
unto those that be of heavy hearts.* And it was said that
compassionate souls in Jerusalem used to donate and
bring these things. But if the women did not furnish
them, at whose cost then were they furnished? It is
quite evident from this that they must be furnished at
public cost.   *(Gemara)*

IF THEY found something for his acquittal, he is set free, but if not he is led out to be stoned. A herald goes before him and calls: So-and-so is being led to be stoned for such-and-such an offense; such-and-such were his witnesses. Anyone that may know anything in his favor shall come and plead for him.   (*Mishna*)

ABAYA said: They must also say: The crime was committed on such-and-such a day, at such-and-such an hour, at such-and-such a place. So that if one can prove that the witnesses testified falsely, he may come and do so.

"And a herald goes before him." This means right before the execution, but not previously.   (*Gemara*)

WHEN he was about ten ells from the place of stoning, they would say to him: Make your confession. That was the way with all who were to be executed. They would make their confession. For he who makes his confession has a share in the world to come.

When he was four ells from the place of stoning they took off his clothes. The men were covered in front while the women were covered front and back. So said Rabbi Yehuda, but the Sages said: A man is stoned naked, but a woman is not stoned naked.

When the flesh was decomposed, the bones were gathered and were buried in their own place. The relatives came and greeted the judges and the witnesses, as if to say: We bear no grudge against you. You have brought in a just verdict. They did not go into mourning for the executed, but they grieved over him, for grief is a matter of the heart.   (*Mishna*)

FROM CHAPTER VI

IF A man breaks into a house, he is judged according to the consequences that might have occurred. If he broke a barrel while breaking in and this caused bloodshed, he is guilty, but if there was no bloodshed he is not guilty.   (*Mishna*)

WHAT is the reason for the law of breaking in? Because a man will surely defend his property. So the thief reasons: If I break in, the owner will surely oppose me and will prevent me from stealing. But if he opposes me, I shall kill him. Therefore the law states: If one wants to kill you, you can forestall this by killing him.   (*Gemara*)

THE following should be saved from committing sin, even at the cost of their lives: he who pursues after his neighbor to kill him; he who is after a male or after a girl who is betrothed. But he who pursues after a beast, he who desecrates the Sabbath or he who commits idolatry, these are not saved from committing sin at the cost of their lives.   (*Mishna*)

FROM CHAPTER VIII

HOW do Abaya and Rab interpret the verse: (*Lev.* xix, 29) *Do not prostitute thy daughter, to cause her to be a whore?* Rabbi Mani says: They mean a man who marries off his daughter to an old man. As we have learned: *"Do not prostitute thy daughter, to cause her to be a whore."*

Rabbi Eliezer says: This means one who marries off

his daughter to an old man. Rabbi Akiba says: This means a man who lets his marriageable daughter sit and wait.

Said Rabbi Kahana in the name of Rabbi Akiba: There is no poor man in Israel except the subtly wicked, and the one who lets his marriageable daughter sit. But is not one who lets his marriageable daughter sit, a subtly wicked man? This is the meaning: Which poor man is subtly wicked? He who lets his marriageable daughter sit and wait.   (*Gemara*)

FROM CHAPTER IX

THE following are strangled: He who strikes his father or his mother; he who steals a soul in Israel; an Elder who rebels against the decision of the court; a false prophet; he who prophesies in the name of a pagan god; he who violates another man's wife, and he who bears false testimony against a priest's daughter and her paramour.

An Elder who rebels against the decision of the court. It was said: (*Deut.* xvii, 8) *If there arise a matter too hard for thee in judgment.* There were three courts. One sat at the entrance of the Temple Mount. One sat at the gate of Temple Court and one sat in the chamber of the Hewn Stones. They would come to the court at the entrance of the Temple Mount and say: So I expounded, and thus expounded my colleagues; so I taught and thus taught my colleagues. If the judges knew anything about the problem, they enlightened them, but if not they went to the court at the gate of the Temple Court, and there propounded their problem. If these judges knew anything about it, they enlightened them. If not,

they all went to the great court at the chamber of the
Hewn Stones whence the laws were issued for the whole
people of Israel.   (*Mishna*)

THE Elder who rebels is guilty of a deliberate sin,
which is punishable by extirpation; but if he sinned
through error, he brings a sin offering. These are the
words of Rabbi Meir. Rabbi Yehuda says: He is guilty
for transgression against a law that is rooted in the
Torah, but its interpretation is made by the scribes.
Rabbi Simon says: He is guilty even for transgressing
only one detail of the interpretation of the scribes.

"Three courts, etc." Said Rabbi Kahana: If the
elder gives a ruling based upon tradition and the court
says: We base our ruling on tradition, he is not executed. If he says: That is how it appears to me and
they say: That is how it appears to us, he is not executed. So much the more if he says: "My ruling is based
on tradition", while they say: "So it appears to us."
IIe is not executed unless he says: "This is how it appears to me", while they say: "We base our ruling on
tradition." This can be deduced from the fact that
Akiba ben Mahalael was not executed. Rabbi Eliezer
said: Though the elder says: My ruling is based on tradition, while they say: This is how it appears to us; he
is executed. Because controversy must not spread in
Israel.

But why was not Akiba ben Mahalael executed? Because he did not give his ruling for the purpose of prac-
tical application. We were taught: So I taught and so
taught my colleagues. Does this not mean that he said:
I base my ruling on tradition and they say: That is how

it appears to us?—No, he said, that is how it appeared to me, while they say, Our ruling is based on tradition.

Come and hear. Rabbi Josiah said: Three things were told to me by Zeira in the name of the man from Jerusalem. When a husband withdraws his warning, it is void. A rebellious son whom the parents are willing to forgive is forgiven. A rebellious elder, whom the court wishes to forgive, is forgiven. But when I came to the South, they agreed to the first two, but they did not agree as to the rebellious elder, because controversy must not be spread in Israel.

At first there were not many quarrels in Israel. The court of seventy-one sat in the Hall of Hewn Stones, and the two courts of twenty-three sat, one at the entrance of the Temple Mount, and the other at the gate of Temple Court. While other courts of twenty-three sat in all cities of Israel. If a problem arose, it was asked of the local court. If they knew of a traditional ruling, they gave it. If not, they asked a ruling from a court in the nearest city. If they knew of a traditional ruling, they gave it; if not, they went to the court at the Temple Mount. If they knew the ruling, they gave it; if not, they went to the court at the gate of the Temple Court. The judges would say: So I expounded and so expounded my colleagues; so I taught and so taught my colleagues. If they knew of a traditional ruling, they gave it; if not, they all went to the court at the Hall of Hewn Stones, where they convened from early in the morning till evening. And on the Sabbath and Festival days they sat on the *hel*. The problem was then stated to them. If they knew the ruling, they gave it to them, if not, they took a vote. If the majority said it was "clean", it was de-

:lared "clean"; if the majority voted "unclean", it was
leclared "unclean". But when the disciples of the Houses
of Hillel and Shamai, who were not very experienced,
multiplied, the quarrels began to spread, and the Law
became like two Laws. From there communications
were written and sent to all places. Whoever was wise
and modest and enjoyed the esteem of his fellow towns-
men was appointed as local judge. From there he was
elevated to the court at the Temple Mount and from
there to the court at the Gate, and from there to the
court at the Hall of Hewn Stones.   (*Gemara*)

MORE emphasis is placed on the words of the scribes
than on the words of the *Torah*. If a man says: There
is no need of phylacteries, he is transgressing a precept
of the *Torah,* and he is not guilty; but if he says the
phylacteries must have five compartments, thus he adds
to the words of the scribes, and he is guilty.

(*Mishna*)

FROM CHAPTER X

ALL of Israel have a share in the world to come,
for it was said: (*Isaiah* lx, 21) *Thy people also shall be
all righteous: They shall inherit the land forever, the
branch of my planting, the work of my hands, that I may
be glorified.* And the following have no share in the
world to come. He that says that no resurrection is
stated in the Bible; he that says that the Bible does not
come from Heaven. The heretic. Rabbi Akiba said:
also he that reads proscribed books, and he that whispers
charms over a wound and says: (*Exodus* xv, 26) *I will
put none of these diseases upon thee which I have brought*

upon the Egyptians: for I am the Lord that healeth thee.
Abba Saul says: He also who pronounces the Name of
the Lord with all of its letters.   (*Mishna*)

SAID Rabbi Yohanan: Where is a resurrection indicated in the Bible?—It was said: (*Numbers* xviii, 28)
*And ye shall give thereof the Lord's heave offering to
Aaron the priest.* Does Aaron live forever? Why, he
did not even enter the land of Israel. Can the offering
then be given to him? This means that he is to be resurrected, and Israel will give him the offering. From this
we infer that resurrection is indicated in the *Torah*. The
school of Rabbi Ishmael taught: To Aaron, means as
Aaron. As Aaron was a scholar, so his sons are to be
considered scholars. Rabbi Samuel ben Nahman said in
the name of Rabbi Jonathan: How do we know that the
offering must not be given to a priest who is ignorant?
(*II Chronicles*, xxxi, 4) *Moreover he commanded the
people that dwelt in Jerusalem to give the portion of the
priests and the Levites, that they might be encouraged in
the law of the Lord.* He who holds to the Law of the
Lord has a share: whoever does not hold to the Law has
no share. Said Rab Aha ben Adda in the name of Rab
Yehuda: Whoever gives the Offering to an ignorant
priest is as if he had given it to a lion. Just as of a lion
we are not sure whether he will tear and eat it, or will
not tear and eat it, so of an ignorant priest we are not
sure whether he will eat it in cleanliness or in uncleanliness. Rabbi Yohanan says: One may even cause him
death. For it was said: (*Lev.* xxii, 9) *And die therefore, if they profane it.* The school of Rabbi Eliezer ben
Jacob taught: He also leads him into transgression, for

it was said: (*Lev.* xxii, 16) *Or suffer them to bear the iniquity of trespass when they eat their holy things.*

Rabbi Simai said: How do we infer resurrection from the Bible?—For it was said: (*Exodus* vi, 4) *And I have also established my covenant with them, to give them the land of Canaan.* It is not said to you, but to them. From this, too, we infer resurrection is indicated in the *Torah.*

Rabbi Gamaliel was asked by the Saducees: Whence do we know that the Lord will resurrect the dead? He answered them: From the *Torah,* the Prophets and the Hagiographa; but they would not accept it. From the *Torah,* for it is written: (*Deut.* xxxi, 16) *And the Lord said unto Moses, Behold, thou shalt sleep with thy fathers and rise up.* But, said they to him: Do we not read: *And this people will rise up?* From the Prophets (*Isaiah* xxvi, 19): *Thy dead men shall live, together with my dead body shall they arise. Awake and sing, ye that dwell in dust: for thy dew is as the dew of herbs, and the earth shall cast out the dead.* Perhaps those are the dead that Ezekiel resurrected? From the Hagiographa, as is written: (*Cant.* vii, 9) *And the roof of thy mouth like the best wine for my beloved, that goeth down sweetly, causing the lips of those that are asleep to speak.* Perhaps this means only that the lips were moving. This is according to Rabbi Yohanan, for Rabbi Yohanan taught, in the name of Rabbi Yehozadak: If a ruling is quoted in the name of one departed, his lips whisper in his grave. For it was said: *Causing the lips of those that are asleep to speak.* Not until he quoted to them the following verse: (*Deut.* xi, 21) *Which the Lord sware unto your fathers to give them.* It is not said to "you",

but to "them". Thus resurrection is stated in the *Torah*.
Others say, he quoted the following verse: (*Deut.* iv, 4)
*But ye that did cleave unto the Lord, your God, are alive
every one of you this day.* As you are alive today, even
though those that live today shall be dead, you will be
alive. As you are alive today, so will you be alive in the
world to come.

Queen Cleopatra asked of Rabbi Meir: I know that
the dead shall be resurrected, for it is written: (*Psalms*
lxxii, 16) *And they of the city shall flourish like grass
of the earth.* Will they arise naked or garbed? He
answered: This is deduced by *a fortiori* argument from
a grain of wheat: While a grain of wheat is put into
the ground naked, it emerges in many garbs. The righteous who are buried in their garments will so much the
more arise dressed.

Caesar said to Rabbi Gamaliel: You say that the
dead will come to life again, but the dead turn to dust.
How can dust come to life again? Said the emperor's
daughter: Let me answer him: We have two pottery
makers in our town. One moulds from water; the other
from clay. Which one is the more praiseworthy? Said
Caesar: The one who moulds from water. If he can
mould from water, he surely can mould from clay, answered his daughter.

A heretic said once to Rabbi Ammi: You say that the
dead will arise again, but the dead turn to dust. How
can they arise again? He answered: I will tell you a
fable: This is like unto a King of flesh and blood who
said to his servants: Go and build for me a great Palace
in a place where there is no earth nor water. They went
and they built him a palace, but in a few days the palace

collapsed. Thereupon the King commanded them to build him a palace in a place where there was earth and water. This we cannot do they said. The King scolded them: In a place where there was no earth and no water, you built a palace; but in a place where there is earth and water you surely can build. But if you don't believe, go into the dale and observe the mouse. Today half of it is dust and half flesh. On the morrow it is all developed, and is entirely of flesh. But if you should say that this takes a long time, go into the mountains and you will find a single snail. On the morrow a rain will fall, and the place will be filled with snails.

A heretic said once to Gebiha ben Pesisa: "Woe unto you, you wicked people! You say that the dead will live again. If even those who are alive shall die, how shall the dead live?" He replied: "Woe unto you, you wicked people! You say that the dead will not live again. If those who do not exist as yet, will live, how much more shall those live who exist now?" "You call me wicked," said the heretic. "If I give you a kick I'll knock the hump off your back." "If you would do that," replied ben Pesisa, "you would be known as a great physician and you would receive a large fee."

THE Rabbis said: There was a story of two men who were taken captive on Mount Carmel, and the captor walked behind them. Said one of them to the other: The camel that is walking in front of us is blind in one eye. It is loaded with two kegs; one is filled with wine, the other with oil. Of the two men that are leading it one is a Jew and one is a heathen. "You stiff-necked people"—said the captor to them—"How do you know all this?" They answered: The camel eats the grass on the side that it can see; on the side it cannot see, it does not eat. It is loaded with two kegs one of wine and one of oil. Wine drips and sinks into the ground, while oil drips and remains on the surface. And the two men that are leading it, one is a Jew, the other a heathen. The heathen attends to his call of nature in the middle of the road, while the Jew steps aside. He ran after them and found that it was really so. He came back and kissed his captives, and made them guests in his home.   (*Gemara*)

FROM CHAPTER XI

Flogging

(Tractate Macoth)

WHAT is to be done with witnesses who testify falsely? If they say of a priest: "We testify that such-and-such a one is the son of a divorcee, or the son of a woman who performed *Halizah,* one cannot say that the false witness should become the son of a divorcee, or the son of a woman who performed *Halizah* instead of the priest, but he receives forty lashes. If they testify that a man should be exiled, one can't say that they should be exiled in his stead, but they receive forty lashes.

If witnesses said: "We testify that so-and-so owes his neighbor two hundred *zuz*" and they were found to have testified falsely, they are flogged and they must, also, pay the sum involved, because the ruling that inflicts upon them the punishment of lashes is other than that which governs their liability for payment. This is the opinion of Rabbi Meir, but the Sages say: If a man is ordered to pay, he is not ordered to be flogged too.

If they said: "We testify that so-and-so is liable to forty lashes," and they are found to have testified falsely, they receive forty lashes in accord with the verse: (*Exodus* xx, 16) *Thou shalt not bear false witness against thy neighbor,* and as many again because: (*Deuteronomy* xix, 19) *Then shall ye do unto him, as he had thought to do.* This is according to Rabbi Meir, but the Sages say: They receive only forty lashes.

Penalties of money are divided among the false witnesses, but the penalty of lashes is not divided. How? If, for instance, they testified that so-and-so owes two hundred *zuz* and it was found that they testified falsely, they divide the fine among them; but if they testified that so-and-so is liable to forty lashes, and it was found that they testified falsely, each one receives forty lashes.

The decisions of the Sanhedrin are valid in the country and outside of it. A Sanhedrin that condemns a man to death once in seven years is considered a destructive body. Rabbi Eliezer ben Azariah said: Once in seventy years. Rabbi Tarfon and Rabbi Akiba said: Had we been members of the Sanhedrin, there never would be anyone condemned to death. Rabbi Gamaliel said: They too would have increased bloodshed.

(Mishna)
FROM CHAPTER I

THE following are banished into exile: Whoever kills someone through an error; for instance: if one was rolling a roof with a roller, and it fell and killed a man, or he was lowering a barrel and it fell and killed a man, or a man was on a ladder and fell on someone and killed him—all these are banished into exile. But if he was pulling up the roller and it fell on someone and killed him, or if one was drawing up a barrel and the rope snapped

and caused the barrel to fall on someone and kill him,
or if one was going up a ladder and fell down on a man
and killed him—All these are not exiled. This is the
rule: Whoever kills someone coming down is banished
into exile; but otherwise, he is not exiled.

If a man threw a stone into a public place and killed
someone, he is banished into exile. Rabbi Eliezer ben
Jacob says: If after the stone has left the man's hand
someone put out his head and it struck him, the man is
not guilty. If a man threw a stone into his own yard and
it killed someone, if that person had the right of entry
into the yard, the man should be banished into exile, but
if the person had no right there the man is not exiled,
for it is written: (*Deut.* xix, 5) *As when a man goeth
into the wood with his neighbor.* . . . The wood is a place
where the injured and the injurer have a right to enter.
From this follows that the yard, into which the other has
no right of entry, exempts the householder. Rabbi Abba
Saul says: This applies to every accidental killing in an
optional act such as the hewing of wood, but it excludes
the father who hits his son, or the teacher who strikes
his pupil, or the clerk of the court who administers the
ashes.   (*Mishna*)

IF HE throws a stone into a public place, is he a de-
iberate offender? Rabbi Samuel ben Isaac said: If it
happens while he is demolishing a wall? Then he should
take precautions. Suppose he was demolishing it at
night,—he should be doubly careful. If he were loading
the debris on a rubbish pile? What sort of a place was
it? If it is a public thoroughfare, then he is guilty of
negligence; but if it is not a thoroughfare, then it is mis-

chance. Rab Papa said: This is a case of a rubbish pile which people are apt to pass at night, but are not using it as a rule during the day time. It so happened that someone came there during the day time. In this instance it is not a case of negligence, because no one is expected there during the day time. It is, however, a case of mischance, because it does occur that people pass it sometimes. (*Gemara*)

A FATHER may escape into exile for the death of his son, and a son may escape into exile for the death of his father. All are banished into exile for the death of an Israelite, and an Israelite goes into exile for the death of all others with the exception of that of a resident stranger. And a resident stranger is exiled only for the death of another stranger. A blind person does not go into exile, so says Rabbi Yahuda, but Rabbi Meir says: He does go. An enemy of the slain man does not go into exile. Rabbi Yosi ben Yehuda says: An enemy should be put to death, because he is a "potential deliberate murderer". Rabbi Simon says: There is an enemy that may escape into exile, and there is an enemy that may not escape. This is the rule: All those of whom it may be said that they killed deliberately, may not escape into exile; but those of whom it may be said that they killed through accident, they may escape into exile.

Whither shall they be banished into exile? To the cities of refuge: To three cities on the other side of the Jordan, and to three cities in Canaan, as it was said: (*Numbers* xxxv, 14) *Ye shall give three cities on this side of the Jordan, and three cities shall ye give in the land of Canaan.*

Rabbi Yosi ben Yehuda said: At first they used to send to the cities of refuge, those that killed deliberately and those that killed through an accident. The court would then send and bring them from there. Whoever was condemned to death was executed, if he were not condemned, he went free; and whoever was sentenced to be banished was returned to the city of refuge, for it was said: (*Numbers* xxxv, 25) *And the congregation shall restore him to the city of his refuge,* etc. . . .

If a man-slayer has escaped to a city of refuge, and the citizens of the town wish to do him honor, he must say to them: "I am a man-slayer." If they answer: "Even so we wish to do honor unto you," he may accept it from them, for it was said: (*Deuteronomy* xix, 4) *And this is the case of the slayer.* They used to pay the salary of the Levites.

Rabbi Meir says: They need not pay them their salaries. He may resume the office that he held before, this is according to Rabbi Meir, but Rabbi Yehuda says: He does not resume his former office.   (*Mishna*)

FROM CHAPTER II

THE following receive lashes: He who has intercourse with his sister, his father's sister, his mother's sister, his wife's sister, his brother's wife, his father's brother's wife, or a menstruant. A High Priest who takes a widow unto him, a priest who takes a divorcee or a *Haluzah,* a layman who takes a bastard or a *Nathina,* or the daughter of a layman who married a bastard or a *Nathina.* If a High Priest married a woman that was a widow and a divorcee, he is liable on two counts, but if he married a woman who is a divorcee and a *Haluzah*, he is guilty only on one count.

He is flogged who eats Holy Food while he is unclean, or he who enters the Sanctuary while he is unclean. He who eats Fat or the Blood, the Remains or the Refuse of Offerings, or that which became unclean, or who slaughtered an Offering outside the Temple, or eats leavened food during Passover, or he who eats or performs work on the Day of Atonement. . . .   (*Mishna*)

WE ARE taught here only of those transgressions that incur death at the hand of the Lord, but not those that incur the death penalty by sentence of the court. The *Mishna* here teaches according to the opinion of Rabbi Akiba. For we have been taught that both those who are liable to death at the hand of the Lord and those who are liable to the death penalty by sentence of the court, incur also the penalty of forty lashes.— These are the words of Rabbi Ishmael. Rabbi Akiba says that only those who are liable to death at the hand of the Lord incur the penalty of forty lashes, for if they should repent, the court of Heaven may grant them forgiveness; while those who incur the death penalty by sentence of the court are not subject to the penalty of "forty lashes", for if they should repent, the earthly court cannot grant them forgiveness. Rabbi Isaac says: Those guilty of incest have already been included in the penalty of death at the hand of the Lord; what reason is there for including here the case of the brother and his sister? —To show that this offense is punishable by extirpation only, and not by forty lashes.   (*Gemara*)

IF A man shears his head bald, and rounds out the
hair on the corners of his head, or shaves the corners
of his beard, or makes an incision into his flesh because
of the Dead, he is liable to forty lashes. . . .   (*Mishna*)

THE Rabbis taught: (*Leviticus* xix, 28) *Ye shall not
make any cuttings in your flesh.* One could believe that
a man is liable to lashes if he cut his flesh because his
house has collapsed, or because his ship was lost at sea.
It is stated (*Ibid.*) *For a soul,*—This means that one
incurs punishment only if he cut his flesh because of the
dead.   (*Gemara*)

IF A man writes on his skin "incision writing" he is
liable to forty lashes. If he wrote but did not tattoo it,
or tattooed but did not imprint it, he is not guilty. He
is liable only if he writes and incises it with ink or with
eye-paint or anything that leaves a permanent mark.
Rabbi Simon ben Yehuda says in the name of Rabbi
Simon: He is not guilty unless he has written the name
of a god. For it was said: (*Leviticus* xix, 28) *Nor print
any marks upon you: I am the Lord.*
    How many lashes are inflicted on a transgressor?
—Forty less one, for it was said: (*Deuteronomy* xxv, 2,
3) *By number forty.* This means a number close to
forty. Rabbi Yehuda says: He gets the full forty; and
where does he receive the fortieth? Between his
shoulders.
    When they estimate how many lashes he can stand, it
must be a number that is divisble by three. If they estimated that he can stand forty, and after he has received
part of the flogging, they say that he cannot stand any

more; he is exempt. If they estimated that he can
stand eighteen, and after he had received the eighteen
lashs they say that he can stand forty, he is exempt from
the rest.   (*Mishna*)

WHENCE is this?—Had it been written: *"Forty in
Number"* I would say it actually means forty lashes
in number, but now that it is written: *"by number forty"*,
it means a number close to forty. Raba said: How fool-
ish are the people who stand up in reverence for the scroll
of the *Torah,* but not for the great men that interpreted
the *Torah.* In the *Torah* it is written forty lashes, but
the Rabbis came, and by their interpretation reduced it
by one.   (*Gemara*)

HOW is a person to be flogged? His two hands are
bound to a post on either side of him, and the beadle of
the synagogue takes hold of his garments.—If they get
torn let them be torn, if they get ripped, let them be
ripped, till his chest is bared. A stone is placed behind
him on which the beadle stands with a strap of calf's
hide, it is folded twice and then folded into four, and
two straps are attached to it. The handle of the strap is
one handbreadth long and one handbreadth wide; and
its tip must reach his navel. He gives one-third of the
lashes in front, and two-thirds behind. He strikes him
neither in a standing nor in a sitting position, but only
when he is stooped over, for it was said: (*Deuteronomy*
xxv, 2) *The judge shall cause him to lie down.* And the
one that strikes, strikes with this one hand with all his
might. And the reader recites: (*Deut.* xxviii, 58) *If
thou wilt not observe to do . . . Then the Lord will make*

thy plagues wonderful and the plagues of thy seed, etc.,
and resumes again from the beginning of the text:
(*Deut.* xxix, 9) *Keep therefore the words of the covenant* . . . and he concludes with (*Psalms* lxxviii, 38) *But
he, being full of compassion, forgave their iniquity,* and
resumes again from the beginning of the text. If he
die under his hand, the man that strikes him is not
guilty. But if he gave him one strike more than was ordered; he must escape into exile. If the person being
flogged befouls himself with feces or with urine, he is
exempt from the rest. Rabbi Yehuda says: A man if he
befouls himself with feces, a woman with urine.

(*Mishna*)

SAMUEL said: If he was tied down, and he man-
aged to escape from the court room, he is exempt. A
question: If he befouled himself at the first or the second stroke, he is exempt. If the strap broke at the second
stroke, he is exempt, but if at the first, he is not exempt.
Why is that? Why should this not be the same as in the
case of his escape—because there he actually escaped, but
in the second instance he really has not escaped.

(*Gemara*)

ALL those who are liable to death at the hand of the
Lord. If they have been flogged, they are exempt from
the punishment of death at the hand of the Lord:
for it was said: (*Deuteronomy* xxv, 3) *Then thy
brother should seem vile unto thee.*—when he has been
flogged, he is considered thy brother. Thus are the
words of Rabbi Hanina ben Gamaliel. Further Rabbi

Hanina ben Gamaliel said: If one commits one sin, he forfeits his soul, how much more, if he performs one precept, shall his soul be restored to him.   (*Mishna*)

FROM CHAPTER III

Oaths

(Tractate Shebuoth)

THERE are two kinds of oaths; these are subdivided into four. Knowledge of being unclean is of two kinds, which are subdivided into four. Carrying burdens on the Sabbath is of two kinds, which are really four. The symptoms of leprosy are two, which are subdivided into four. (*Mishna*)

NOW, the author has just finished the tractate "*Macoth*", why does he begin with the tractate of "Oaths"?—Because there he taught: For the cutting of the hair around the corners of the head one is punished with two lashes, one for each side. For the shaving of the beard one is punished: twice for each side of the face and once for under the chin. Because he is discussing here one transgression that merits two punishments, therefore he continues with two kinds of Oaths, that are subdivided into four.—Why does the author treat only here, of all the laws of "two that are subdivided into

four"? Why didn't he treat of the carrying of burdens
on the Sabbath and of the symptoms of leprosy in the
tractates where they belong?—I will tell you: The laws
of oaths and knowledge of being unclean are mentioned
in the Bible in the same place, and are similar to each
other in that they merit a "Rising and Falling Offering".
The author then began here with the laws of oaths, and
also with the laws of uncleanliness, and having treated
of them here, and since there are but a few of these laws,
he disposes of all of them here at one time. Then he pro-
ceeds to the laws of oaths, which are many.

There are two kinds of oaths, these are subdivided
into four. Two: I shall eat; I shall not eat. These are
subdivided into four: I have eaten; I have not eaten.
There are two kinds of knowledge of being unclean,
which are subdivided into four. Two: The knowledge
of being unclean while eating holy food, and the knowledge of being unclean while having entered the sanctuary.
These are subdivided into four: Knowledge of being unclean, and knowledge of eating holy food, knowledge of
being unclean, and knowledge of entering the sanctuary.

The symptoms of leprosy are two, which are subdivided into four. A boil and a bright spot. The boil and
its species and the bright spot and its species.

Who is the author of this *Mishna?*—It is not Rabbi
Ishmael, nor is it Rabbi Akiba. It is not Rabbi Ishmael
for he says that only one who makes an oath in the future
tense is liable. And it is not Rabbi Akiba who says: He
is liable only if he forgets that he is unclean, but is not
liable if he forgot that he entered the sanctuary.

If you wish I may say that the author of this *Mishna*
is Rabbi Ishmael, and if you wish I may say that it is

Rabbi Akiba. It may be Rabbi Ishmael, for one is liable
for some of the oaths, and is held not liable for other
oaths. And it may be Rabbi Akiba, for again for some
of the oaths one is liable, while for others one is not liable.—How not liable? Does not the author teach of all
of them, together with the laws applying to the symptoms
of leprosy: just as in these, one is liable in all the four
subdivisions, so in the case of oaths, is not one liable in
all instances?—Indeed, the author is probably Rabbi
Ishmael; and though in the case of the oaths, he does
not hold liable one who made the oath in the past tense,
he frees him only from bringing a sacrifice, but he holds
him liable to lashes. This is in accord with Raba, who
said: The *Torah* plainly states that a false oath is the
same as a vain oath; just as a vain oath is of necessity
in the past, so also is a false oath in the past tense.
The author of this *Mishna* is its compiler, Rabbi. In
one instance he accepted the opinion of one of the Rabbis,
while later on he adopted the decision of a different
Rabbi.   (*Gemara*)

FROM CHAPTER I

IF ONE said: "I swear that I shall not eat", and he
ate and drank, he is liable only once. If he swore: "I
shall not eat and I shall not drink", and he ate and
drank; he is liable twice. If he swore that he would not
eat, and he ate a piece of wheaten bread, and a piece of
barley bread, and a piece of bread made of spelt, he is
liable only once. If he swore that he would not eat wheat
bread, barley bread, and spelt bread, and he ate them, he
is liable for each one of them separately.

If he swore that he would not eat, and ate things

which are not fit to be eaten, and he drank liquids which are not fit for drinking, he is not held liable. If he swore that he would not eat, and ate carrion, or unkosher food, or forbidden animals, or reptiles, he is liable. But Rabbi Simon says: He is not liable. If he says: *"Konam* (sacred); I shall not enjoy my wife if I have eaten to-day"*, and he ate carrion, unkosher food, forbidden animals, or reptiles, his wife is forbidden to him.

(*Mishna*)

RABBI Hiya ben Abin said in the name of Samuel: If a man said: "I swear I shall not eat," but he drank, he is guilty. If you wish, I can prove it to you by logic and if you wish I can prove it to you from the *Scriptures*. If you wish, I can prove it to you by logic, for if one says to his friend: "Let's partake of something" they go in and eat and drink. And if you wish, I can prove to you from the *Scriptures* that drinking is included in eating. For it was said: (*Deuteronomy* xiv, 23) *And thou shalt eat before the Lord thy God, in the place which he shall choose to place his name there, the tithe of thy corn, of thy wine.* *Tirosh* is wine, and yet it is written: *"Thou shalt eat."* Possibly the *Scripture* means when one dips his bread in it. For Samuel said: Wine sauce is prepared with almonds and juices of other vegetables. Furthermore Rabbi Aha bar Jacob explained: Can this be deduced from the following verse: (*Deuteronomy* xiv, 26) *And thou shalt bestow that money for whatsoever thy soul lusteth after, for oxen, or for sheep, or for wine, or for strong drink.* Wine is a drink, yet here "eating" is used.—Perhaps it means in wine sauce? It is said "strong drink" which means something that intoxicates.

And perhaps a pressed fig is meant, for it was taught:
If he ate a pressed fig and ate honey and milk and had
then entered the Temple and performed the service, he
is liable.—Furthermore we deduce that drinking includes
eating, from the words "strong drink" which is used in
the case of the Nazirite, just as it means wine there, so
it also means wine here.   (*Gemara*)

WHAT is a vain oath?—If he swore of something
that is contrary to what is well known to all men. For
instance: he said of a pillar of stone that it was of gold;
he said of a man that it was a woman or of a woman
that it was a man. Or if he swore of a thing that was
impossible: "If I have not seen a camel flying in the air,"
or "If I have not seen a serpent as thick as a beam of
the olive-press." If a man said to witnesses: "Come
and testify for me" and they replied: "We swear that
we will not testify for you." If he swore that he would
nullify a precept, if he said I shall not erect a hut on the
Feast of Tabernacles, or I shall not take a *Lulab* on the
Feast of Tabernacles, or I shall not put on phylacteries.
These constitute a "vain oath", for which he is liable
to lashes, if he uttered them deliberately, but if he uttered
them unwittingly he is not guilty.
   If a man swore: "I shall eat this loaf of bread,"
then he swore: "I shall not eat this loaf of bread." The
first is "a rash oath", the second is "a vain oath". If he
ate it, he transgressed a "vain oath", if he did not eat
it he transgressed a "rash oath".   (*Mishna*)

ULLA said: This applies to something that is known
to at least three persons. If one swore of a thing which

is impossible: "If I have not seen a camel flying in the air." What is meant by: "If I have not seen"? Abaya says: Read: "I swear that I have seen." Raba said: It means a man said, "All the fruits in the world should be forbidden to me if I have not seen a camel flying in the air." Said Rabbina to Rab Ashi: It may be that the man saw a large bird, and he called it a camel, and when he swore, he swore according to what was in his mind. But if we say, we go according to what he utters with his mouth and not according to what is in his mind. It is not so. For we were taught: When a man was adjured, they said to him: "Know that we adjure you not according to what is in your mind, but what is in our mind and in the mind of the Court." Why is this? Because it may be said, that a man gave to his debtor chips and counted them as *zuzim*, and when he swore, he swore according to what was in his mind.—Not so, for this is the case of Raba and the cane. (A man was sued for a sum of money which was loaned to him. He was brought before Raba. Just as he was to go on the witness stand he handed his cane to the plaintiff and asked him to hold it for him. Whereupon he swore that he returned the money. The plaintiff got so angry that he broke the cane in his excitement; behold! money fell out of the cane. It was then established that one swears not to what is in his mind, but what is in the mind of the court.) (*Gemara*)

THE laws regarding a "rash oath" apply to men and. to women, to relatives and to those who are not relatives, to those who are qualified to be witnesses, and to those who are not. It matters not whether the oath was made before a court or not, as long as it was uttered from the person's own mouth. And if it was uttered deliberately, he is liable to lashes, but if unwittingly he brings a "Rising and Falling Offering".

The laws of "a vain oath" apply to men and to women, to relatives and to non-relatives. To those who are qualified to be witnesses and to those who are not. It matters not whether the oath was uttered before a court or not, as long as it was uttered by one's own mouth. If it was uttered deliberately he is liable to lashes, but if unwittingly, he is exempt. For either of these oaths, if he was adjured by others, he is liable. Thus if he said, I have not eaten today, and I have not put on phylacteries today, and one said to him: "I adjure you", and he said, "Amen", he is guilty.   (*Mishna*)

FROM CHAPTER III

AN OATH concerning testimony applies to men, but not to women. It applies to strangers but not to relatives, to those that are fit to bear witness, but not to those who are unfit, to those who are qualified and to those who are not qualified. It matters not whether the oath was uttered before a court or not, but it must be uttered from a man's own mouth; if he was adjured by the mouth of others, he is not guilty, unless he denies it before the court. This is according to Rabbi Meir. But the Sages say: Whether he uttered it from his own mouth, or he was adjured by the mouth of others, he is not liable unless he denies it before the court.

One is guilty if he swore deliberately, or if he swore unwittingly, but deliberately denied the knowledge of testimony. But he is not guilty if he denied it in error.

And what is one liable for a deliberate oath? He is liable to a Rising and Falling Offering.

What is an oath of testimony? If a man called two persons and said to them: "Come and bear witness for me" and they swore that they knew of no testimony for him, or if they said that they knew of no testimony for him, and he said: "I adjure you", and they said "Amen", then they are guilty. If he adjured them outside the courtroom five times, but when they came before the court they admitted the knowledge of testimony, they are exempt. But if they denied it, they are guilty for each oath. If he adjured them before the court five times, and they denied, they are guilty only once.

(*Mishna*)

FROM CHAPTER IV

WHAT is an oath of deposit? If a man said: "Give me my deposit that I have with you" and the man swore: "You have nothing with me", or if he said: "I have nothing that belongs to you", and the other said: "I adjure you", and he answered: "Amen", he is guilty. If he adjured him five times, before a court or not before a court, and he denied it, he is guilty on each count. Rabbi Simon said: What is the reason? Because he can retract and admit each time.

If one said: You have violated, or you have seduced my daughter, and the other said: "I have not violated", or "I have not seduced your daughter", and he said "I adjure you"—and he answered "Amen" he is guilty. Rabbi Simon exempts him. For a man does not pay a fine through his own admission. But though he pays no fine on his own admission, he still pays for the blemish, or for the indignity that he caused through his own admission.

If a man said: "You have stolen my ox" and the other answered: "I have not" and he said: "I adjure you" and he replied "Amen", he is guilty. If he said: "I stole it, but I have not killed it, nor have I sold it", and the other said: "I adjure you", and he replied "Amen" he is exempt.

There was a rule established. Whoever must pay a fine through his own admission is liable; but if he does not have to pay a fine, he is exempt.

"YOU have violated, etc." . . . What is Rabbi Simon's reason? Because the claimant is mainly seeking the fine. Raba said: According to Rabbi Simon this could be compared to the case of a man who says to his neighbor: "Give me the wheat, the barley, and the spelt that I have with you", and the other says: "I swear that you have no wheat with me", and it is proven that he had no wheat with the man, but barley and spelt he did have; he is exempt, for he swore that he had no wheat and that was true. Said Abaya: Can this be compared? Here he denies the possession of wheat, but does not deny the possession of barley and spelt, while there he denied the whole thing. But this then is to be compared to one who says to his neighbor: "Give me the wheat, the barley, and the spelt that I have with you." And the other answers: "I swear that you have nothing with me", and it is proven that he has barley and spelt, but he had no wheat; he is liable. When Rabbin came he said in the name of Rabbi Yohanan: According to Rabbi Simon, he is asking only for the fine, but not for the shame and blemish that he caused. But according to the Sages, he is claiming both the fine and also quittance for the shame and the blemish.—Where is the disagreement?—Rab Papa said: Rabbi Simon is of the opinion, that a man does not leave that which is fixed for something which is not fixed, while the Rabbis are of the opinion that a man does not leave that for which if one were to admit it, he would not be exempt, for that for which if he were to admit it, he would be exempt. (*Gemara*)

FROM CHAPTER V

ALL those who are made to take an oath as prescribed in the *Torah,* swear and need not pay. The following take an oath and collect that which they claim: The hired man, one who has been robbed, one who has been wounded, and the one whose defendant cannot be trusted to take an oath, and the storekeeper on his account book. For instance if a hired man said: "Give me my wages that are due me", and the man answered him: "I have given you your wages", and the hired man says: "I have not received any." He takes an oath and obtains his wages. Rabbi Yehuda says: Not unless the claim was admitted in part. How?—If for instance he said to him: "Give me my wages of fifty *denars* that are due me", and he answered: "You have already received one golden *denar."* How about a man that was robbed? If it was testified that a man entered the house without permission, to take a pledge, and the owner says: "You have taken my vessel", and the other answers: "I have not taken", the owner takes an oath and receives his vessel. Rabbi Yehuda says: Not unless there was partial admittance. If he said: "You have taken two vessels," and the other replied: "I have taken one." . . .

How about the storekeeper on his books? Not if he says: "There is an entry on my books that you owe me two hundred *zuz*." But if he said, for instance: "Give to my son two *selahs'* worth of wheat", or "give to my labourers a *selah's* worth of change", and he says I have given it to them, while they say that they have not received it. The storekeeper takes an oath and obtains his due, and they take an oath and receive their due. Ben Nanas said: How is that? They both are made to take a "vain oath". No, he gets his without an oath, and they get theirs without an oath.

If a man said to the storekeeper: "Give me a *denar's* worth of fruit", and he gave it to him and then said: "Give me the *denar*", and he replied: "I have given it to you and you put it into your till." The householder takes an oath that he gave the *denar* to the storekeeper. If the householder says "Give me the fruit," and the storekeeper says: "I have given them to you and you took them home", then the storekeeper takes the oath. Rabbi Yehuda says: He that is in possession of the fruit, has the upper hand.

If a man said to a money changer: "Give me a *denar's* worth of change" and he gave it to him and then the money-changer says: "Give me the *denar*", and he replies: "I have given it to you and you put it into your till", then the householder takes an oath. If the householder gave him a *denar*, then asks him for the change and the money-changer says: "I have given it to you, and you put them into your purse." Then the money-

changer takes an oath that he gave him the change.
Rabbi Yehuda says: It is not the way of a money-
changer to give even an *issar* without first receiving the
denar.   (*Mishna*)

"ALL THOSE who are made to take an oath, etc."
Where do we deduce this?—For the *Scripture* said:
(*Exodus* xxii, 11) *And the owner of it shall accept
thereof, and he shall not make it good.* He that has to
make the payment, he is the one to take the oath.

"The following take an oath and collect." Why is a
hired-man different, that the Rabbis have decreed that
he should take the oath and obtain his payment? Said
Rab Yehuda in the name of Samuel: Here they taught
a great law. Are these then laws? Say then, that these
are great rulings—Great, because there are also minor
rulings? But Rab Nahman said in the name of Samuel:
They enacted here iron-clad laws. The Rabbis here took
the oath away from the householder and imposed it upon
the hired man for the sake of his livelihood.—Shall we
then injure the householder for the sake of the livelihood
of the hired man?—the householder himself would prefer that the hired man take the oath and get his wages,
so that the men will hire themselves out to him.—Just
the opposite. Would not the hired man prefer that the
householder take the oath and be freed from paying him,
so that the householder be compelled to hire him?—The
householder has to employ hired men. The hired man
needs employment.—Furthermore the householder is occupied with his many hired men.—Then why should he
not pay him without an oath?—Just to appease the house-

holder—Then why should he not pay him before witnesses?—That would be inconvenient for him—Then
why should he not pay him at the beginning?—Well, both
need credit. This should also apply in the case of arranging the amount of the wages stipulated. Therefore
we have learned: If the labourer says: You stipulated
two *zuz;* while the householder says: "I stipulated only
one", the burden of proof falls upon the one who de-
mands the payment. The labourer surely remembers the
amount stipulated.—If so, this should also apply in case
the time of payment has expired. Why was it taught:
If the time had expired, and he did not pay him, he does
not take an oath to receive his wages?—It is assumed
that the householder will not transgress the precept:
(*Lev.* xix, 13) . . . *shall not abide with thee all night until the morning.*—But didn't you say that the householder is preoccupied with his hired men?—This only before the time of payment has arrived. But when the
time of payment has arrived? The obligation lies heavy
upon him and he is aware of his duty.—Will the labourer
then transgress the precept: (*Lev.* xix, 13) *Thou shalt
not rob?*—As for the householder there are two assump-
tions: First the householder will not transgress the precept regarding the *wages of a hired servant,* and second,
the hired man will not allow the payment of his wages
to be delayed.   (*Gemara*)

FROM CHAPTER VII

THERE are four kinds of guardian: an unpaid guardian, a borrower, a paid guardian, and a hirer. The
unpaid guardian takes an oath in every instance, and is
exempt; a borrower must pay in every instance; a paid

guardian or a hirer takes an oath in case the beast was injured, was captured, or died, and he is exempt; but he must pay if it were lost or stolen. (*Mishna*)

FROM CHAPTER VIII

GLOSSARY

Amora (pl. *amoraim*), interpreter, teacher, sage of the *Talmud* after the Mishnaic Age.

Baraitha, external.

Denar (pl. *denarim*), a silver, or gold coin.

Gemara, lit. completion, also study. The commentary on the *Mishna.*

Haggada (pl. *haggadoth*), homiletical portions of the *Talmud,* legend.

Halacha (pl. *halachoth*), traditional law, ruling.

Halizah, rite performed by a childless widow (*Deut.* xxv-9).

Haluzah, childless widow who performed the rite of *Halizah.*

Hanukah, the festival of the Maccabean.

Haroseth, a mixture of nut fruit and wine.

Issar, a copper coin 1/24 of a *denar.*

Kab, measure of capacity 1/6 of a *seah,* 4 *loogs.*

Kilbith, a very small fish.

Konam, sacred, a term introducing a vow.

Kor, a measure of capacity = thirty *seahs.*

Loog, a liquid measure 1/4 of a *Kab.*

Lulab, palm branch.

Maneh, a weight in gold = 100 *zuz.*

Midrash, interpretation of Scriptures, exposition.

Minah, 100 *Denars.*

Mishna, lit. "teaching," the collection of traditional laws.

Mezuza (pl. *mezuzoth*), a rolled up piece of parchment containing *Deut.* vi, 4-9, xi, 13-17, put on the door post.

Nathin, f. *nathina,* descendants of the Gibeonites whom Joshua made into Temple slaves. (*Josh.* ix-27).

Omer, first sheaf of barley offered as a meal offering to the Temple. (*Lev.* xxiii-10).

Pandion, coin 2 *issar*.

Peah, corner of the field.

Perutha, the smallest copper coin 1/8 of an *issar*.

Ris, a measure of distance 266-2/3 cubits.

Sanhedrin, supreme court.

Seah, measure of capacity 1/30 of a *Kor*.

Selah, a coin 4 *denars*.

Shekina, the spirit of the Lord as manifested on earth.

Sinar, a girdle, apron.

Sotha, wife suspected of adultery.

Sukah, a hut, a booth used during the Feast of Tabernacles.

Talmud, lit. study, learning, *Mishna* and *Gemara*.

Tanna (pl. *Tannaim*), a teacher, sages of the *mishnaic* times.

Torah, the Law, the Pentateuch.

Tropaik, 1/2 denar, 1/2 zuz.

Urim athumin, Oracle.

Zuz, another name for *denar*.